THE SCHOOL BUDGET:

It's Your Money; It's Your Business

by

Rhoda E. Dersh

Published by

The National Committee for Citizens in Education
Suite 410, Wilde Lake Village Green
Columbia, Maryland 21044

First Printing
September 1979

ISBN No.–0–934460–10–8

Library of Congress Catalog Card Number 79–90677

MANUFACTURED AND PRINTED IN THE UNITED STATES OF AMERICA

About the Author

RHODA DERSH had worked with other parents for improved educational programs in her children's public schools for years before being named the League of Women Voter's observer to the local school board. She then recognized how critical the board's budget-making process was to quality programs in the district.

As a delegate to the 1970 White House Conference on Children, she became aware of the universal nature of many problems involved in school budgets and improved programs throughout the country. After years of intensive study and meetings with people from various parts of the United States, she became director of the nonprofit Public School Budget Study Project in 1975.

With a grant from the Educational Foundation of the American Association of University Women, she researched school budget issues in 47 states involving 250 school districts. This study resulted in the publication of a widely distributed guide designed to help citizens better understand and participate constructively in the school budget process. The guide has been recommended or used by the Harvard Graduate School of Education, *The American School Board Journal,* United Press International, as well as study groups from many AAUW, League of Women Voters, PTA and other citizen groups.

Through workshops, lectures, articles and consulting engagements, Rhoda Dersh has continued to help citizen groups and school districts improve the process of shared decision making in school budget matters.

Today, living in Green Hills, PA. with her family, she is a management consultant. She has continued as the consulting director of the Public School Budget Study Project in Reading, PA., serves as the 1979–1980 president of the American Academy of Independent Consultants in Philadelphia, and is recognized in the 1979–1980 *Who's Who of American Women* for her professional and voluntary public service.

Acknowledgements

T HE ORIGINAL encouragement for this effort was given by the Educational Foundation of the American Association of University Women (AAUW) and resulted in *The School Budget is your Business* published in 1976. That book was selected by NCCE as the basis for *The School Budget: It's Your Money; It's Your Business.* The author recognizes with appreciation the support of AAUW, the interest of NCCE, and the valuable "observer" experience provided by the League of Women Voters which sparked the author's interest in school improvement projects.

Both the first book and this revised edition received ideas and assistance from many parents, school officials, friends and family. The author especially recognizes the encouragement and support from Dr. Jerome Dersh, Debby Dersh and Jeff Dersh, as well as Chrissie Bamber, Richard Cahn, Carl Marburger, Bill Rioux and Stan Salett. NCCE recognizes the contribution of members of their staff and citizen groups who critiqued the manuscript and made many valuable suggestions. These include Nancy Gross, Beverly Norbeck, Terry Peterson, Richland District I Parents Forum, Columbia, S.C.; Carl Richman, Seattle, WA.; Bill Rosenbloom, St. Paul (MN) Citizens for Better Education; and Grace and Ted Ruscitti, Hopewell Area Citizens Association, Aliquippa, PA.

TABLE OF CONTENTS

Chapter 7
The Budget Worksheets: Finding the Facts in the Figures

Chapter 8
Citizen Strategies

SAMPLE LETTERS

BUDGET WORKSHEETS

BUDGET EXCERPTS

CHARTS AND ILLUSTRATIONS

Contents—(Continued)

Contents—(Continued)

Chapter 1
Why the School Budget is Your Business

I F THERE IS ONE thing citizens all over the United States have been saying loudly and clearly for the past few years it is that we believe the way the government spends our money is *our* business. The so-called "taxpayers' revolt" is, in part, an outcry against inflation and the cost of government services. As taxpayers, we may be the providers of government services, but as citizens, we are the consumers of these services. And as consumers, we have a real and strong interest in the quality of the services and in the way they are run. So it is only right that we should take an active interest in their operation.

In no area has this feeling been expressed more strongly than in education. In the past, most parents and citizens were content to leave the operation of the public schools entirely to the professionals. That is hardly the case today. Before 1972, the bylaws of the National Congress of Parents and Teachers (PTA), the oldest nationwide parent group, stated that local chapters should "cooperate with their schools in ways that will not interfere with the administration." Since 1972, the bylaws have stated something very different: that local PTA groups should "seek to participate in the decision-making process establishing school policy." Nor is the PTA the only group concerned with this issue. All kinds of parent/citizen organizations all over the country are taking an active interest in educational policy making and in the day-to-day operation of their children's schools.

This means that citizens are taking—or at least *should* be taking—an active interest in the school budget—and not only because it's our money that makes up the budget, but for other reasons, too.

There is, for example the question of the value we are getting for our educational dollars. Every school budget contains just so much money, and what is spent in one area can not be spent in another. Every school budget reflects a set of choices and values—it represents the list of priorities that has been established for the district's schools. If you want to be sure that good education for children is at the very top of that priorities list, you *must* be concerned with the school budget.

Note that we said "good education." For the school budget reflects more than the quantity of money that goes into educating your children. It also reflects the quality of that education and the plans your district has for carrying it out. Those plans were probably made at professional meetings and conferences in which you, as a member of the public, did not participate. But if you know how to look at a school budget—how to ask the right questions about it and how to follow up on those questions—you will be able to discover what the plans are and what they mean for the quality of education in your district. And if either needs improvement, you'll have the information you need to bring that improvement about.

The budget is your business for still another reason. It reflects the quality of management in the local schools. If the budget itself is disorganized and sloppy—if it is difficult for you to find the answers to such simple questions as "How much did we spend last year on athletic programs?" "How much will we spend for remedial reading this year?"—you can be pretty sure that the school management is disorganized and sloppy, too. This certainly would suggest that money was being wasted, and also might suggest that education was suffering—if only because it is difficult for teachers and students to do their best in schools that are badly run.

There's still another reason for you to be concerned about the school budget. Many people who are professionally involved in education—teachers, school administrators, school board members and others at every level of government—both want and need your help. In the course of preparing this book, we wrote to a large number of school districts asking, among others, the question: "Do you encourage citizen participation in your budget process?" Of the 230 districts that responded, seven answered "no," and six offered answers that indicated little enthusiasm for citizen participation. But the overwhelming majority—217—said "yes," they want the citizens in their communities to participate in school budget making. In fact, some states require such participation and in others the state boards of education distribute manuals and other publications designed to acquaint parents and citizens with the process by which the school budget is drawn up. Moreover, federal law requires that parents be involved in the planning, development, operation and evaluation of several educational projects. Such involvement may not always be effective, but it *is* required by law and parents who are concerned to see that the law is translated into useful action can take the steps that are necessary to ensure that their voices are heard.

Finally, the school budget is your business because, as a responsible citizen, it is your obligation not only to participate in the democratic process but to do everything you can to assure the continuation of that process—to assure that democracy will function tomorrow as well as or better than it does today. That means participating in the system that is a significant part of your children's life and is training your children for that future—the public schools. And that, in turn, means understanding the school budget. More than any amount of conversation or discussion, more than any number of meetings or conferences, the budget tells you about the quality of education in your community's schools.

Understanding a school budget can be a difficult task, taking lots of time and effort, but it is not impossible, as many parents and citizens think. The school budget *can* be demystified: that is the purpose of this book. We may not be able to answer every single question that occurs to you or even point you towards an answer to that question. Education is a state function in our country, and different states have different laws and regulations relating to the educational budget. There is no single standardized budget form, no single way of preparing the budget, no single rule concerning citizen participation in the budget process; there isn't even a single set of terms or accounting code numbers that are uniformly used for school budgets throughout the country. But even with these limitations, we believe that you will find this book a help. Once you have some understanding of the budget and are no longer intimidated by it, you will be able to move ahead on your own, to tackle your community's specific school budget problems, and to work to make changes where you think them necessary.

All you need is the willingness to work, a pocket calculator, and the conviction that the school budget *is* your business—that it is too important a matter to be left in the hands of the "experts" and the bureaucrats, and that parents and citizens can, and should, play a significant part in making their school budget work for their community and their community's children.

Chapter 2

What Can You Learn from the School Budget?

THE QUESTION that provides the title for this chapter is an important one, and it deserves a serious answer. For the fact is that parents and citizens who undertake a study of the school budget have a real job ahead of them—not only because budgets and the process by which they're arrived at are complicated in themselves, but also because it is often difficult simply to get hold of the materials you need in order to conduct a budget study. So if the job is to be worthwhile, it has to have some payoff. You have to be able to learn things from a study of the budget and to be able to do things as a result of studying it that you neither would know nor be able to accomplish otherwise. There are such things, and this chapter will indicate a few of them—not only to give you an idea of the benefits of budget study, but to provide a framework that will enable you better to understand and apply the specific, how-to information with which much of the rest of this book will be concerned.

First, as to what you can learn from the budget: the document itself, whether it is long or short, well organized or not, contains the answers to a number of questions. The answers are not always easy to dig out, even for those with training and experience in the field. If a budget has been deliberately designed to confuse the reader—to conceal information that the budget-makers, for one reason or another, do not want you to have—no amount of effort or expertise will make it comprehensible. On the other hand, the very fact that a budget cannot be unravelled answers a very important question about the people who made it up. It tells you immediately that they may have had something to hide. But if the budget makers go about their task with honesty and some degree of professional know-how, you should be able to find, in the document they produce, some very important information.

You will not find it merely by reading through that document. You have to know how to study and analyze it, and how to make comparisons—between your district's budget and the budgets of districts similar to yours; between your district's current budget and its budgets for preceding years; among items in its various sections. One of the purposes of this book is to tell you how to make these analyses and comparisons: we will discuss this subject in detail in Chapter 7. We also will discuss other aspects of the budget that you will have to know about—the policies, politics and practices that underlie it and the process by which it was arrived at (Chapter 6): you also will need to know these things if you are to be able to make the changes you feel are necessary.

But now, let us concentrate on the kinds of information budget study can supply, if only to give you some idea both of how wide-ranging and how specific this information can be and of the number of aspects of educational, political and pocket-book issues it can cover.

On the whole, the information can be broken down into two categories—the hard facts and the interpretive or soft ones. The hard facts are those that everyone agrees on, no matter how he feels about them. The interpretive ones are much less firm. The district superintendent, the president of the teachers' union, the leader of a parent/citizen group and the head of a taxpayers' organization—each is likely to give you a different answer to the same soft question. Most of the hard facts can be found in the budget document itself. Some of the interpretive facts also can be found there, but they often concern state and local politics and policies as well, and are related as much to the process by which the budget is arrived at as to the final document.

Hard Facts

Below is a list of some of the hard facts that can be discovered by studying the school budget. It is only a partial list, and the questions about it may or may not be relevant to your particular interests. Its purpose is not to be exhaustive or authoritative, but to indicate the scope of the questions to which budget study can reveal the answers. By studying your school budget you can learn a lot about your school district, its priorities, and the education it's offering your children.

- Are you going to be paying higher property taxes next year in order to support the school budget?
- Is the federal government's share of your school's expenses the same as last year's or less? What about the *state's* share?

- Has an increase been budgeted for next year for the special education program your parent/citizen group convinced the school board to endorse as a top priority item? How large is that increase?

- Which programs will be getting less money next year? Which programs will be getting more? What new programs are being added?

- What objectives does the budget specify for the advanced placement science program in the high school?

- Do the estimated or anticipated expenditures for the current year coincide with the budget figures adopted at the beginning of the year?

- Do the proposed figures increase or decrease the teacher-to-pupil ratio in secondary school classrooms?

- How many more (or fewer) teachers, administrators, janitors, or students are included in this year's budget than were included in last year's?

- How much is the district planning to spend on remedial reading programs at the elementary, junior high school, and high school levels?

- What programs in the budget are mandated by the state and/or federal governments?

- Who is responsible for preparing the budget?

- Is the district planning to spend more on maintenance and less on the elementary school counselling program?

- Does the budget include money for items such as Astroturf for the football field?

- How much does your district allocate per pupil for administrative purposes?

As you can see, these questions are of various sorts, and can produce various kinds of answers, ranging from a simple "yes" or "no" through dollar figures to long essays on educational goals. But whatever the answers, they are not matters of interpretation or opinion. Whether one approves or disapproves of the answers, whether one asks the district superintendent or the president of the teacher's union, the answers remain the same.

Soft Facts

This is not true of the interpretive facts. These involve value judgments, individual and organizational priorities, and differing points of view, and the questions that relate to them do not have simple, factual answers. But the issues they involve—the way a school district functions; how and why educational decisions are made; what the quality of administration and management are in the local schools; how much power various groups exert in the budget-making process—are equally as important as the issues that produce hard fact answers.

Below is a list of some of the questions whose answers will give you interpretive facts. As in the case of the hard facts, you will be able to think of many others.

- Why is the school budget increased by only 5% while the mass transit system budget increase is 12%?

- On what basis did the school budget officer recommend increasing the property tax rather than the sales tax in order to provide additional money for the school budget?

- Is your local school district receiving a fair share of the state's money for schools? Does the state formula for school aid take such issues as property-poor communities, municipal overburden, and density factors into consideration?

- Did the parents have any input in determining the budget for the schools? If they did, was it before or after cuts and additions were made?

- Why are reductions recommended in the music, art and library programs while negotiations on teachers' salaries are still going on?

- Were last year's objectives for the language program fully met?

- Why has your school district been fighting for—or against—a new distribution formula for state or federal education money? Or—why hasn't it been fighting?

- How can parents have some input into the budget process early enough so that they are not forced into the futile exercise of a last minute public hearing?

- Why was additional money transferred into the maintenance budget instead of the library after the budget was adopted for the current year?

- How was the study of the district's educational needs conducted and how are the results reflected in the current budget?

- How is the list of goals and priorities for the school district reflected in the current budget?

- Why does the budget list only the amount that was budgeted for the current year rather than the amount that is actually being spent?

Putting the Information to Good Use

Once you have received answers to the questions you've raised, the next question comes up: What can you do about the budget, and about the answers that are unsatisfactory to you? Here's a short, illustrative list:

- You may want to work to eliminate unnecessary programs. You may want to work to include an especially promising program. You may want to reduce or raise the budget allocation for one or more programs.

- You may want to press the school board and the administration to present a cost/benefit analysis of certain programs. You may want to see the studies the administration conducted before deciding to include new administrative positions in the budget or press for such studies if they were not conducted.

- You may want to work to change the budget process so that you and other parents can get in on the ground floor—long before the board, the teachers and the administrators have already defined the turf they are going to fight for. You may want to press to move up the date of the public hearing on the budget so that there is enough time for the board to consider parent/citizen reactions to the proposed budget before adopting it. You may want to change the closed-door process by which the school district presents the budget to the county or city council.

- You can work to change the budget figures—on specific programs or on specific line items. You can work to distribute information about the budget and the budget process to fellow citizens. You can work to make the figures, the budget document and the budget process more understandable and more open to the public. You can work to set up an observer corps that will monitor commitments that may be made this year that will lock in expenditures for next year!

- You can work to change the composition of the school board and the school administrations if their decisions and/or management produce a budget that you and other parents cannot live with. You can support a new school board slate or run for office yourself, so that you can help make the final budget decisions. You can serve on the local site board so that you can help make the decisions that affect your own school.

- You can work to change the effect of some of the outside pressures on your local school district—commitments to raises for personnel that have been legislated by the state; provisions for programs which are not adequately funded by the federal government; provisions that collective bargaining be conducted in secret; and many other commitments and provisions, mandated by the state and federal government, that restrict the flexibility of your local school district. (You also can study the details of such mandates to ascertain whether your school district is using some of them as excuses for "business as usual.")

You can, in other words, do many things about the school budget—and, therefore, about education—in your school district. What you can do is in fact limited only by the depth of understanding you gain through your budget study, by the time and persistence you are prepared to commit to it, and by your ability to persuade and work with other parents and citizens to be certain that the budget document, the budget process, and the entire school system reflect the community's interests. It's your money. It's your school system! It *is* your business.

Chapter 3

The School Budget: What Is It?

THERE IS NO single answer to this question. Every school district, whether large or small, has several school budgets. There is the Proposed Budget, (Illustration 1, page 14) in which the superintendent sets forth his suggestions for the coming year. There is the Tentative Budget, generally derived at least in part from the superintendent's proposals, which is adopted by the school board and used as a basis for discussion in reaching the final budget. There is the Popularized Budget, designed to inform parents and citizens about the budget in general terms before it becomes final. Sometimes it consists of no more than a newsletter outlining the superintendent's proposals. Sometimes it is considerably longer and contains several pages of explanation, a general summary and a few specific figures (Illustrations 2 and 3, pages 15 and 16). And finally, there is the budget document itself—the sheaf of papers drawn up each year to detail the district's financial and educational plans for the forthcoming year. Even this document is not a single budget. It's usually composed of several: an Operating or General Fund Budget, which covers expenditures made from the General Fund, and separate budgets for such services as Food and Transportation funded through other sources, and a Capital Expenditures Budget which covers the cost of building new facilities, renovating old ones, and in some cases purchasing expensive equipment.

Just as there is no single school budget, so there is no single way in which the final budget document appears. Every state prescribes the format its local districts must use, but these formats (Illustrations 4 and 5, pages 18 and 19) vary widely from one state to the next. One thing virtually all of them have in common, however: they were not designed with us in mind. The guiding principle behind them has nothing to do with whether the general public can understand them, but with the ease with which they fit into the state's accounting system.

For this reason, many school districts do not use the state's required form during the course of their debate, discussion, and adoption of the budget—and, in fact, no school district should. Instead, they modify it by adding the kind of information school board members, staff, and the public must have if they are to be able to understand the budget and participate in the process by which it is developed. Many districts, for example, prepare a detailed program budget, specifying and spelling out such individual programs as Third Grade Remedial Reading; Ninth Grade Chemistry; etc. Only after all these specific items have been debated, modified, and adopted are the figures translated into the terms the state requires—terms that frequently make little sense to anyone seeking a real understanding of the way school money is being spent.

This is the first and most important lesson for you to learn. Whatever form the school budget takes in your state, it is bound to be far from ideal. It probably will not include everything it ought to, and probably will not be written in a form that is easy to understand. But even though it is doubtful that an ideal school budget document exists anywhere, you should know what such a document could contain. Only in that way will you be able to make an informed judgment about the adequacy of the school budget in your own district.

A Well-Prepared Budget Document

Every school budget should contain four essential components:

1. **A Revenue Plan,** sometimes called "receipts" or "income."

2. **An Expenditure Plan,** also called "allocations," "expenses," etc.

3. **An Educational Plan,** including the goals and objectives of the school district and the programs included in the budget. It is sometimes integrated with the Expenditure Plan.

4. **A Priority Plan** (this section, which identifies the priorities that have been adopted by the board, is often included in the Educational Plan).

The Revenue Plan: *the part of the school budget which should list the moneys the school district expects to receive and all the sources from which these moneys will come.* This listing should be quite detailed. It should include, for example, the amount to be received from the local property taxes, from local income or sales taxes, from tuition for summer school programs. There should be comparative figures for each item listed: how much was actually received from each source last year; how much was budgeted for the current year; how close to that figure the actual receipts for the current year will be, based on the amount already received; how much is budgeted for the forthcoming year.

The assessed value of the real estate in your school district and the property tax millage rate should be specified for the forthcoming year and for the two comparative years—this year and the preceding one. Increases and decreases in receipts for state and federal programs should be clearly indicated. There should be explanations of the way the state's contribution to the budget was figured. The number of pupils on which the state's formula is based should be indicated. If the state's contribution is figured on a weighted basis, there should be an indication of how many elementary school students, weighted as perhaps 1, are anticipated next year as compared to the number of secondary students, weighted at 1.5. It should be indicated whether the state's contribution is based on Average Daily Membership (ADM), or Average Daily Attendance (ADA).

The Expenditure Plan: *generally the place where the most extensive detail is found.* Often the proposed expenditures are presented in both a program and a line-item format. A well-prepared budget will group expenditures according both to local program categories and to the specific line items required by the state and prescribed by the state's Accounting or Financial Manual, a document that includes a Chart of Accounts indicating the way expenditures are to be grouped within the state's designated categories (Illustration 21, page 63).

The local program categories should be identified as specifically as possible—Third Grade Science: Lincoln Elementary School; Vocational-Technical Upholstery Program: North Center High. Within each program, the budget should list the amounts to be spent on salaries for teachers, for administration, for supplies, for overhead. It should list the program's per-pupil cost—sometimes called the unit cost—so that you can see differences, if they exist—if, for example, the Third Grade

Illustration No. 1
PROPOSED BUDGET

200—EXPENSES OF INSTRUCTION

	Actual Expenditures 1975-76	Estimated Expenditures 1976-77 June 30, 1977	Budget 1976-77	Proposed Budget 1977-78
Salaries for Instruction				
211—Principals				
1001—Elementary Principals (6)	124,200	134,200	133,770	142,350
2001—Secondary Principals (7)	159,815	167,850	168,630	178,550
211—TOTAL SALARIES—PRINCIPALS	284,015	302,050	302,400	320,900
212—Directors (2) _002 _050				
—Learning Resources, Special Ed.	43,074	47,050	47,500	47,850
213—Elementary Teachers				
—Regular Classroom Teachers (91)	1,383,682	1,395,230	1,452,000	1,416,200
1001—Special Subject Teachers (13.8)	176,135	181,582	184,472	187,800
1002 (Reading—2.8; Art—3.5; Music—4; P.E.—3.5)				
1061—Title I	51,349	51,000	50,000	63,500
1041—Academically Talented Program (12)				
(one additional teacher)	170,000	169,220	171,700	190,700
1004—Team Leaders—(2); Sub. Contracts	146,122	141,000	142,290	147,000
1051—Special Education (12); Team Leader (1)	36,000	33,000	33,200	38,200
1003—Instructional Aides (14 — ½ days)	7,200	8,100	8,100	9,000
1004—Team Leaders—Supp. contracts (18)				

Detailed proposed Budget Section on Instructional Expenses,
Excerpt, Marple Newton (PA) School District, 1977-1978 Proposed Budget. p.5.

Illustration No. 2
POPULARIZED BUDGET

COMPARATIVE SUMMARY 1974–75 AND 1975–76

	CURRENT 1974-75	PROPOSED 1975-76	DIFFERENCE	± %
A. Instruction Salaries of all teachers, substitutes, aides, professional specialists, principals, assistant principals, supervisors, directors, coordinators, and secretarial personnel; classroom and office supplies, instructional materials, library materials, and other expenses related to regular and special instructional programs.	12,236,095	14,070,895	+ 1,834,764	+ 14.9
B. Operation Salaries of custodians, grounds keepers, and vehicle operators; supplies for operations; garbage removal and other contracted services; heat and all utilities	1,412,125	1,973,325	+ 561,200	+ 28.4
C. Maintenance Salaries of maintenance personnel, materials for building repair, painting, modification; all new instructional, custodial, health and maintenance equipment	1,057,243	1,337,763	+ 280,520	+ 26.5
D. Fixed Charges Costs mandated by law including social security, retirement funds, property and employee insurance.	1,090,147	1,203,000	+ 112,853	+ 10.4

Illustration No. 3
POPULARIZED BUDGET

EXPLANATION OF INCREASES

Each of the major budget categories are affected by the approximately 6% increase in enrollment and the inflation experienced by all of us in costs of basic supplies, materials, and equipment amounting in some cases to as much as 10%.

A. Instruction +14.9%

Increased costs for paper, pencils, books, audio visual materials, and other instructional supplies are readily apparent. Negotiated salary adjustments and the addition of twenty (20) teachers to handle increased enrollments also contribute to increased costs in this area.

B. Operation +28.4%

This account reflects salary increases of approximately 4%, great increases in utilities costs (approximately 33%), and supplies which in all areas cost at least 10% more than they did last year. No personnel increases are anticipated; continuation of current service is provided.

C. Maintenance +26.5%

Contractors have increased their charges by at least 15%. Costs for materials have risen sharply. In order to carry out the District's long range maintenance plan detailed in the complete budget proposal, anticipated costs are reflected in this area. It must be remembered that with the exception of the new Middle School and some additions to buildings completed in the 1950's and early 1960's, most of our schools are well over 50 years old and are in need of constant major maintenance efforts.

D. Fixed Charges +10.4%

This account anticipates increased Board contributions to Social Security because of raised contribution levels recently enacted by Congress. Insurance rates have increased in proportion to increased property valuations and coverage needed for the new 10 million dollar Middle School.

East Orange, New Jersey "The 1975–76 Proposed School Budget Summary

Science Program at Lincoln Elementary School is budgeted as $136 per pupil, while the same program is budgeted at $79 per pupil at Washington School (Illustration 6, page 20).

The local program budgets also should contain the figures indicating what was actually spent on each individual program last year, what was budgeted for the program this year, and how close this year's actual expenditures are to the budgeted figures. This information should be presented next to each line item of the forthcoming year's program budget, so that the differences are clearly visible.

The expenditure plan also should summarize proposed expenditures according to function and object. For example, all the administrative costs, for all the programs, should be totalled, so that you can tell the amount being spent on administration throughout the district. The Administration category also should be broken down to indicate how much is being spent on salaries, on materials, on clerical assistance, on legal, business, and other expenses. Each of these figures should be lined up next to comparative figures: what was spent last year, what was budgeted for the current year, how close the expenditures for the current year are to the budgeted amount.

Some of the details that are part of the expenditure plan may be included in appendices or schedules that should form part of the budget. For example, a well-prepared budget will contain an appendix on teacher's salaries (Illustration 7, page 21) that indicates the various steps in the salary schedule; an appendix on student enrollment that indicates how many pupils are and will be enrolled in each grade in every school in the district. It will contain an appendix on staffing guidelines, (Illustration 8, pages 22 and 23) indicating such facts as, for example, that there is to be one teacher for every 22 third-grade students, one library specialist for every 250 students, one reading supervisor for every ten reading specialists. There should be an appendix on expense guidelines (Illustration 8, pages 22 and 23) that tells you if textbooks are budgeted at $2.40 per elementary pupil this year as opposed to $2.13 last year; if $5.02 per pupil has been allocated for equipment replacement in the secondary schools and $1.67 per pupil in the elementary schools.

The budget also should include individual budgets for each school building or each geographic area, (Illustration 9, page 24) along with figures from last year's budget and actual expenses for that area or school. The figures budgeted for the programs within the schools should be accompanied by the figures for prior years.

Finally, in a well-prepared budget, any significant differences—more or less than last year; a greater or lesser proportionate increase or decrease—will be explained in notations or footnotes (Illustrations 1 and 3, pages 15 and 16). If, for example, there is a significant reduction in teachers' salaries for the reading program in a given school, the budget should contain an explanation of this fact. Perhaps the reduction is accom-

Illustration No. 4

STATE REQUIRED PUBLIC SCHOOL BUDGET FORMAT

Submit in Duplicate To:

Chief, Public School Finance Division
Department of Finance and Administration
State Capitol Building
Santa Fe, New Mexico 87503

STATE OF NEW MEXICO

PUBLIC SCHOOL BUDGET
1975-1976

EXPENDITURE CLASSIFICATIONS		ACTUAL EXPENDITURES 1973-74	NO. OF PERSONS UNITS OF TENTHS	ESTIMATED EXPENDITURES 1974-75	NO. OF PERSONS UNITS OF TENTHS	*ALL OTHER NON-OPER. BUDGETS	NO. OF PERSONS UNITS OF TENTHS	PROPOSED OPERATIONAL	NO. OF PERSONS UNITS OF TENTHS	APPROVED AT HEARING	FINAL APPROVED BUDGET
		1	2	3	4	5	6	7	8	9	10
1.XXX ADMINISTRATION											
1.1XX Salaries—Administration											
Superintendent	1.110										
Administrative Associates	1.120										
Administrative Aides	1.130										
Secretary Clerical/Technical	1.140										
1.3XX Purchased Services—Admin. Audit	1.310										
Legal Services	1.320										
Election Expense	1.330										
Bond Retirement Fees	1.340										
Other Purchased Services	1.390										
1.4XX Supplies & Matls.—Admin. General Supplies and Matls.	1.400										
1.5XX Travel-Administration Travel	1.500										
1.9XX Other— Board of Education Board of Education Dues	1.930										
Board of Education Travel	1.950										
Board of Ed.—Other Expense	1.990										
1.XXX Series Sub Total											

*Complete separate line item budget on authorized budget form (PSF Budget Form 2) for each program.

Illustration No. 5
STATE REQUIRED POLICIES & PROCEDURES

CDE-HNB-F01   Section No: ACC/301   Page 3

Date Issued: **July 1, 1975**   Effective Date: **January 1, 1976**

Subject: **THE "EDUCATIONAL ACCOUNTABILITY ACT OF 1971"
and the "FINANCIAL POLICIES AND PROCEDURES ACT"**

Basic Procedures

1. **Planning:** improve statement of goals and write learner, staff, and program objectives.

   Planning begins with the refinement of district goals for students and with the identification of initial student needs relative to the established goals. Once the goals and needs have been developed, the next step is to write learner, staff, and program objectives. The objectives state what the learner is to do, what the staff is to do, and what the program (yet to be decided) is to accomplish.

2. **Programming:** develop alternative new program or proposed methods for improving existing programs—citing anticipated results and anticipated costs in achieving the desired objectives.

   Program structure should clearly show the relationship between student goals and objectives in a hierarchy where anticipated costs/results and actual costs/results can be determined, aggregated, and evaluated in increasingly larger units.

3. **Budgeting:** analyze the actual costs/results of current programs in terms of the district's goals and objectives and relate actual costs/results to anticipated costs/results of alternative new programs or changes of methods.

   It now becomes the responsibility of the business offices to allocate funds based on the established priorities. When proposed programs or changes of methods cannot be afforded, they will have to be reworked by the educational program planners, and other alternatives will have to be re-appraised. Programs related to low priority goals and objectives may have to be dropped. The decisions are not easy. However, a systematic, analytic procedure for relating priorities of student goals and objectives to priorities of anticipated cost-effective programs does facilitate program budgeting, rather than budget programming. Such a procedure is sensitive, at every step of the process, to the educational needs of the community.

4. Determine Results/Evaluation: modify programs and methods based on relating actual results to actual costs.

   After a program has been in operation for a period of time sufficiently long enough to get results, educational results can be related to costs. Value judgments can then be made as to whether or not educational programs and methods are doing what they were designed to do at justifiable costs. This is the point where program strengths and weaknesses can be identified. Using this information as a basis for planning completes one cycle of program budgeting and starts another.

Colorado Department of Education "Financial Policies and Procedures" p.3.

Illustration No. 6

BUDGET-PROGRAM SUMMARY ANALYSIS

FAIRFAX COUNTY PUBLIC SCHOOL SYSTEM
1977-78 SUB-PROGRAM SUMMARY ANALYSIS
FUND—SCHOOL OPERATING FUND NO. 04

AS OF 7/01/77

PROG NO-F1980

$ IN THOUSANDS—PERSONNEL ACTUAL

NO	SUB-PROGRAM DESCRIPTION	1975 ACTUAL AMOUNT	PERS	1976 ACTUAL AMOUNT	PERS	1977 ESTIMATED AMOUNT	PERS	1978 SUPT BUDGET AMOUNT	PERS	1978 APPROVED BUDGET AMOUNT	PERS
100	GENERAL INSTRUCTION	$64,928.4	5293.5	$72,503.4	5342.9	$68,774.6	4827.1	$69,370.1	4758.5	$72,201.2	4782.8
101	MUSIC	1,740.5	158.7	1,975.4	161.1	2,122.2	159.0	2,919.9	148.9	2,008.4	242.6
102	KINDERGARTEN	2,249.7	190.8	3,654.5	350.5	3,335.5	300.5	2,286.0	151.0	1,920.9	242.0
103	PHYSICAL EDUCATION	2,649.7	155.8	3,511.5	150.0	1,787.6	151.6	1,826.4	151.0	2,368.6	147.0
104	SPECIAL READING	1,786.1	146.5	2,107.6	151.5	2,204.8	153.0	2,238.1	153.0		153.0
107	PUPIL SUPPORT	981.9	64.0	1,278.7	79.0	1,778.3	113.5	1,980.6	122.5	2,212.9	127.5
111	MATHEMATICS			6.4		.9		.4		.0	
112	SCIENCE	14.5		3.5		.0		.8		4.8	
113	BUSINESS EDUCATION	14.7	1.0	146.2		120.0	1.0	125.6		131.9	
114	HEALTH & PHYSICAL EDUCATION	420.8	22.0	509.6	22.0	522.4	22.0	506.2	22.0	537.7	22.0
116	FINE ARTS INSTITUTE			24.4				.3		20.5	
118	VOCATIONAL EDUCATION	1,851.3	129.0	2,328.4	138.5	8,928.5	547.1	9,226.1	545.0	10,083.9	552.6
119	MEDIA SERVICES	3,289.9	209.5	3,547.3	209.5	3,700.1	2045	3,686.6	204.5	3,872.9	203.5
120	GUIDANCE	4,015.7	293.0	4,500.9	294.5	4,635.8	293.0	4,877.5	290.0	5,175.5	293.0
121	ACCREDITATION	34.3		3.8							
122	STUDENT ACTIVITIES	1,045.2	843.5	1,176.3	853.0	1,253.5	846.3	1,351.5	838.3	1,351.5	837.7
123	ADMINISTRATION	18,745.6	1119.0	13,709.7	1079.0	14,086.1	1096.5	13,925.0	1104.0	14,625.7	1104.0
124	PLANT OPERATIONS			19,817.6		22,060.4		22,010.0		23,010.7	
126	TUITION GRANTS/CONTRACT SERVICE	1,492.0		1,519.7	3.0	2,456.1	3.0	3,256.5	3.0	3,399.3	3.0
127	LEARNING-DISABLED/ELEMENTARY							2,776.6		2,833.5	
128	MODERATELY RETARDED	436.8	48.0	494.1	55.0	489.3	53.0	534.3	49.0	513.3	46.0
129	MILDLY RETARDED	800.6	61.0	947.7	61.0	613.1	61.0	813.3	61.0	861.3	60.0
130	PHYSICALLY HANDICAPPED	480.5	38.5	447.8	44.0	445.7	48.0	514.9	51.5	540.8	50.5
131	GIFTED AND TALENTED	216.2	18.0	291.1	20.0	419.0	24.0	541.8	25.0	564.2	25.0
132	SPEECH	1,006.4	79.0	1,208.6	98.0	1,273.8	98.0	1,289.2	98.0	1,286.8	96.0
133	VISION	124.7	10.0	139.4	11.0	152.6	11.0	156.9	11.0	167.0	11.0
134	LEARNING-DISABLED/SECONDARY	2,245.6	188.0	3,415.7	259.0	4,166.6	353.0	1,400.6	122.5	1,234.6	122.5
135	GENERAL ADULT	181.9		181.9		45.7		45.7		1,223.7	
136	ADULT HIGH SCHOOL	316.4	24.0	421.9	26.0	478.9	26.0	462.7	25.0	489.1	25.0
137	ADULT BASIC EDUCATION	127.9	6.0	89.4	6.0	137.0	5.0	154.3	4.0	150.7	4.0
138	APPRENTICESHIP	77.6	2.0	84.6	2.0	104.8	2.0	115.5	2.0	119.1	2.0
139	ADULT DISTRIBUTIVE EDUCATION	46.0	1.0	61.9	1.0	54.4	1.0	35.8		66.4	1.0
140	TRADE EXTENSION	11.0		30.1	1.0	130.6	1.0	113.0		148.0	1.0
141	CAMP 30	39.3		39.1							
142	HEARING-IMPAIRED	405.7	41.0	611.7	55.0	765.0	64.0	894.1	83.0	906.0	82.0
143	HOMEBOUND INSTRUCTION	175.9		141.8		141.7		150.2		157.7	
143	FIRE CONTROL	4.8		6.7		7.8		10.0		10.0	
144	SUPPLY	894.7	71.0	978.3	42.0	871.9	68.0	893.7	68.0	939.2	68.0
145	MAINTENANCE OPERATIONS	6,895.9	498.0	7,463.6	496.0	8,430.8	496.0	8,937.6	495.0	8,435.6	498.0
146	TRANSPORTATION	5,594.1	715.0	5,447.1	689.0	7,618.6	724.0	7,230.0	777.0	7,728.5	778.0
149	EMPLOYEE BENEFITS	8,937.6		13,334.7		18,108.6		23,626.7		22,783.2	

CHART 20

Detail of Fairfax County Public School System 1977-78

Budget, showing planned expenditures on a program by program basis. Fairfax County, 1977.

Illustration No. 7

BUDGET DETAIL: PROFESSIONAL SALARY SCHEDULE

PROFESSIONAL SALARY SCHEDULE
(Effective July 1, 1979)

STEP	ND 10-Month	GRADE A BA 10-Month	GRADE B BA+15 10-Month	GRADE C MA/MA EQ 10-Month	GRADE D MA+30 10-Month
1	$ 7,589	$11,003	$11,551	$12,323	$13,202
2	7,920	11,661	12,213	13,092	13,973
3	8,250	12,323	12,871	13,862	14,743
4	8,581	12,982	13,532	14,633	15,513
5	9,791	13,643	14,192	15,402	16,281
6	10,232	14,303*	14,852	16,174	17,053
7	10,780	14,963	15,513	16,942	17,824
8	11,221	15,624	16,174	17,712	18,592
9	11,772	16,284	16,834	18,484	19,363
10	12,323	16,943	17,383	19,254*	20,134*
11	12,762			20,025	20,906
12	13,312			20,794	21,675
13				21,565	22,445
14				22,335	23,214
L1				22,885	23,765
L2				23,435	24,315
L3				23,985	24,865

*Maximum entrance step
——— Schedule to continue for personnel employed prior to 7-1-75
- - - - Applicable for personnel employed 7-1-75 and after

Illustration No. 8
STAFFING AND EXPENSE GUIDELINES FOR BUDGET

STAFFING AND EXPENSE GUIDELINES

Elementary and Secondary School Ratios
Bylaw 313:1 dated May 27, 1964, Maryland State Board of Education

The classroom teacher is the key member of the professional staff, and the degree of teacher time which is available to students for instructional purposes is a major index of educational quality. In recognition of the fact that the appropriateness of a specific ratio of pupils to each classroom teacher may vary in relation to such factors as subject requirements, pupil characteristics, and school size, no prescriptive and detailed ratio is set forth herein. In staffing schools with classroom teachers, however, school administrators should regard ratios ranging from *one classroom teacher for each 28 pupils to one for each 25 pupils* as the arrangement which will be approximated following assignment of all professional personnel in the local school system. Each elementary school should be staffed with or have available resource personnel in order to provide a comprehensive program of instruction in all areas of the curriculum.

STAFFING GUIDELINES

A. ELEMENTARY

School Enrollment	Assistant Principal	Media Specialist	Instr. Material Aide	School Sec. III	School Sec. I
Under 250			1		
2500- 599		1	1	1	0.5
600 - 799		1	1	1	1
800 - 999	1	1	2	1	1.5
1000 -1199	1	1	2	1	2

School enrollment means students in Head Start, Kindergarten, Grades 1–12 and Special Education. Each pupil shall be counted as one for purposes of the guidelines.

Illustration No. 8 (Continued)

EXPENSE GUIDELINES

	Budgeted FY1979	Recommended FY1980
Instructional Equipment—Per Pupil (Additional)		
Elementary (K–6)	$1.00	$1.06
Middle/Junior	1.25	1.32
Senior	1.35	1.43
Instructional Equipment—Per Pupil (Replacement)		
Elementary (K–6)	1.58	1.67
Middle/Junior	3.17	3.36
Senior	4.74	5.02
Textbooks—Per Pupil		
Elementary (K)	2.13	2.40
Elementary (1–6)	7.81	8.82
Middle/Junior	11.26	12.72
Senior	11.26	12.72
Materials of Instruction—Per Pupil		
(Includes supplies for classroom instruction, media center, health room and school office)		
Elementary (K–6)	17.42	19.16
Middle/Junior	30.65	33.71
Senior	32.41	35.65
Media Center Collection		
Additional Materials for Existing Schools		

A minimum library book collection of 5,000 books per school or 10 books per pupil in schools over 500 based on the pupil enrollment of the school, and three non-print items of instructional materials per student.

Illustration No. 9
GEOGRAPHICAL AREA BUDGET

BUDGET WORKSHEET

			GENERAL FUND	INSTRUCTION PROGRAM		WEST AREA ORGANIZATION	
OBJECT	DESCRIPTION	1975-76 ACTUAL	1976-77 ACTUAL	1977-78 BUDGET POS.	1977-78 BUDGET	1978-79 REQUEST POS.	1978-79 REQUEST BUDGET
400-04	Area Superintendent	$ 37,440	$ 38,882	1.0	$ 40,895	1.0	$ 38,948
400-06	Director, S.E.A.	32,290	—	—	—	—	—
402-20	Principals, Elementary	534,531	556,635	39.2	1,123,656	41.7	1,290,596*
402-21	Principals, Secondary	757,301	765,206	—	—	—	—
402-24	Principals, Special Assignment	57,519	68,793	1.0	36,827	1.0	37,798
403-30	Teachers, Kindergarten	477,594	506,916	—	—	—	—
403-31	Teachers, Elementary	4,381,077	4,655,700	709.7	12,404,674	628.5	12,040,803*
403-34	Teachers, Secondary	6,806,450	7,378,790	—	—	—	—
409-09	Teachers, Other Administrator	13,778	—	—	—	—	—
409-17	Teacher, Resource	32,072	—	—	—	—	—
405-44	Librarians	409,591	423,739	23.0	435,029	24.3	461,168*
452-62	Clerical	776,289	847,758	83.7	838,866	81.8	826,998*
406-47	Social Worker	7,130	10,928	—	—	—	—
451-65	Teacher Aides	770	—	—	—	—	509,034
401-08	Project Administrator—Bryant Y.E.S.	22,150	—		see page 24		see page 24
412	Principals, Extended Assignment	60,579	117,599	—	—	—	10,300
413	Teachers, Extended Assignment	14,036	8,721	—	—	—	2,733
415-44	Librarians, Extended Assignment	3,446	2,479	—	2,720	—	—
419	Other Certificated, Extended Assignment	2,000	—	—	—	—	—
462-62	Clerical, Extended Assignment	7,232	5,564	—	5,199	—	5,150
492-62	Clerical, Overtime	601	2,467	—	4,752	—	2,750
459-99	Non-Certificated, Other	532	—	—	—	—	—
469-99	Student Help	3,517	1,835	—	—	—	2,000
	Staff Development, Salary	23,515	15,515	—	38,000	—	37,600
	TOTALS	$ forward	$ forward		$ forward		$ forward

*Includes Staff Utilization

Excerpt—The 1978-79 Adopted Budget, Minneapolis Public Schools panied by the addition, at the same cost, of a new program in remedial reading at that school. Perhaps two experienced teachers are retiring and are to be replaced by two new teachers whose lower salaries account for the savings.

The Educational Plan: *should specify what the district's overall goals are (Illustration 10, page 28) and detail what programs at what cost have been designated to meet those goals.* It is often integrated into the expenditure plan. There should be specific descriptions of the objectives for each program and of the criteria by which the success of the program will be judged (Illustration 11, page 29). The expenditures for each program should be broken down so that you can see exactly what amount is to be spent on professional salaries, on teacher aides, on textbooks, on travel expenses, on consultants, etc. And, as noted above, each of these figures should be presented with the comparative figures from last year and the current year (Illustration 6, page 20).

The specific educational plan for the year ahead should be discussed in terms of the district's long-range educational plan, and should indicate how its objectives tie in with these longer-range goals. It should indicate which programs are required by the state and which by the federal government and which have been identified as necessary by the local school district and community. The plan should indicate the standards that are to be met in each program and should list these standards in terms of outcomes, inputs, and the processes to be used.

If, for example, individualized reading is to be instituted in Lincoln School and one-to-one teacher aide programs are to be used in the Washington School reading program, the budget should tell you the specific costs of each program, the specific outcomes to be achieved, and the criteria to be used in evaluating them. You also should be able to see how each of the programs fits in with such overall educational goals as building self-sufficiency or cooperative spirit among the students.

The Priority Plan: *a ranking of each existing program and its objectives in relation to other proposed expenditures.* Options are spelled out to help school boards and communities commit resources to programs which meet the greatest local needs in the most cost-effective way. The Priority Plan also aids decision making when program changes are considered due to an altered budget picture.

The priority plan should be based on a needs assessment developed by school personnel, parents, students, and the community (Illustrations 12 and 13, pages 30 and 31). It also should be based on state and federal requirements and on policies adopted by the local school governing body. The priority plan should summarize the needs assessment and indicate where one can go to examine that document. It should specify the procedures by which it was determined and detail the policies adopted by the board of school directors that established the priorities it lists.

SAT scores, achievement test scores, and trends may be included in a priority plan. It also may include material that formed the basis for setting certain priorities: accreditation agency reports on the high school; state building inspector reports; library or teacher association reports.

If the budget process in the school district is properly organized, the priority plan will be included from the very earliest stages of budget planning. It will, in other words, form part of the proposed or tentative budget. This makes it possible for every citizen in the school district to see where cuts, if they are necessary, are likely to be made. If the priority plan is modified by official action of the board at the time the annual budget is adopted, the new priority plan should be made widely available. If some unanticipated revenue is realized during the year, the priority plan will make it clear where such revenue should go; if some cost savings are realized in one program or budget category during the year, the priority plan will indicate where the funds should be transferred.

*　　　*　　　*　　　*　　　*　　　*　　　*

This, then, is what a budget should look like. It should include a Revenue Plan, an Expenditure Plan, an Educational Plan, and a Priority Plan—spelled out in detail and accompanied by supporting schedules or appendices. It should have a table of contents and an index; a list of the names and telephone numbers of the persons to whom citizens can address questions about the various portions of the budget; and a list of the names and locations of the specific documents that support the budget figures. And, most important: even before the table of contents, the budget document should have an introduction—or budget message—that helps make the budget understandable. The introduction should call attention to the assumptions that underlie the budget; should point out the major differences between the document and the ones for preceding years; should indicate where additional information can be found; and should offer any other information the reader will need in order to understand the document itself (Illustration 14, pages 32 and 33).

Illustration No. 10
BUDGET LONG-RANGE GOALS

The goals of education for the Montgomery County Public Schools are set forth in this statement of public policy to guide the school system in developing, implementing, and improving educational programs for its students. This statement outlines those goals considered by the citizens of the county as most important for the education of their children in public schools and for which the citizens will hold the school system responsible and accountable.

The school system has the primary responsibility for some of these goals. For others, it shares that responsibility with the home and other community institutions.

The extent to which these goals can be realized will depend upon the endorsement by and continuing commitment of the school system staff, students, parents, and the community. With broad endorsement and wide support, the Montgomery County Public Schools will continue its development to serve its students and community in the most effective way possible.

Education is a process that encompasses the total experiences of each individual throughout a lifetime of formal and informal learning. The school program, as a keystone in this process, should provide opportunities and encouragement for students to acquire knowledge, to explore ideas, to ask questions, and to seek answers that will lead to sound and useful conclusions.

The probability of success motivates students to learn. Each school must create a program and maintain a climate in which every student has opportunities for success. Each individual is unique, and the school shall encourage that uniqueness. The school should help the student understand his values and the values of others.

The school program, while developing the skills of learning, should be based on the study of broad human concerns, flexible enough to deal with changing concerns and at the same time related to the needs, interests, and concerns of each student. The program should offer opportunities for decision-making. It should help the student develop the capacity to learn throughout his lifetime, to respond to and understand other human beings, and to accept full responsibility for the results of his actions.

Therefore, the Montgomery County Public Schools dedicates itself to provide the opportunity, encouragement and guidance to make it possible for every child to attain the following goals of education:

The Goals of Education

ACADEMIC SKILLS

The fundamental responsibility of the school is to develop programs that enable each child to acquire those skills basic to all learning. The achievement of all other goals depends upon the success of the school in ensuring that each student according to his own abilities, attain the following basic skills.

- **Reading:** The ability to read and comprehend written material and relate it to other knowledge

- **Composition:** The ability to write with precision, clarity and acceptable usage, whether to inform, inspire, or persuade

- **Listening and Speaking:** The ability to listen attentively and with understanding and to speak with confidence and effectiveness, whether from written material or extemporaneously

- **Mathematics:** The ability to perform computations and solve common problems of mathematics and logic, and to understand the structure of mathematics so it can be a useful tool in daily living

- **Study:** The development of basic study skills so that he may acquire knowledge efficiently

- **The Arts:** The development of some of the basic disciplines and skills in the performing and creative arts to be used throughout his life for communication, expression, and enjoyment

- **Observation:** The ability to identify and differentiate elements of the world around him as they are useful to personal, academic, and artistic pursuits.

PHYSICAL DEVELOPMENT

Each person matures physically at a different rate and possesses differing capabilities. The school has the obligation to help each student:
- understand the biological functioning of his body
- make the best both of physical talents and limitations
- develop good health habits, skills, and interests to maintain his body in optimum condition throughout his lifetime.

INTELLECTUAL DEVELOPMENT

In addition to acquiring academic skills, each individual should develop his intellectual capabilities to the fullest extent possible. Therefore, the school will encourage each pupil:
- to think creatively
- to reason logically
- to apply knowledge usefully
- to deal with abstract concepts
- to solve problems

Portion of the budget discussion guide, CHOICES FOR OUR CHILDREN, indicating the Long Range Goals of the Montgomery (MD) County Public Schools.

Illustration No. 11

PROGRAM BUDGET GOALS AND OBJECTIVES

DEPARTMENT OF ALTERNATIVE CENTERS—547
Special Education and Related Services: Mark Twain School
Unit/Program Name and Budget Code

COMPONENT DESCRIPTION

Title

Special Education and Related Services: Mark Twain School

Program Description

The Mark Twain School serves seriously emotionally disturbed students whose needs cannot be met in the regular school program. It helps students modify inappropriate school behaviors and develop academic skills so they can return, within two years, to a regular Montgomery County school program.

All students receive daily instruction in English, math, science, social studies, and physical education. Students also have the opportunity to participate in laboratory experiences in art, drama, home economics, music, and industrial arts. Each student is assigned to a teacher/advisor who is responsible for developing a close supportive relationship with student and parents. The teacher/advisor conducts group counseling sessions three to five times per week for his/her eight to ten advisees.

Parent involvement is an integral part of the Mark Twain Program. Parent classes meet during school days, in the evenings, and on Saturdays and Sundays. The groups help Mark Twain parents to understand and take an active role in the development and implementation of each student's individualized educational program.

Mark Twain is actually three separate schools. The Upper School serves 50 students in Grades 9, 10, and 11. The Middle School serves 90 students in Grades 6, 7, and 8. The Lower School serves 100 students in Grades 6, 7, and 8. The alternatives in each school range from self-contained classrooms to interdisciplinary teams of teachers who work with a large group of students.

In addition to the 240 students served at Mark Twain School, 60 students are served at the Junior and Senior High School Satellite Centers. These students receive the intensive support provided by the Mark Twain staff but have the opportunity to be mainstreamed into the regular educational program at the host school. Another alternative program is the Twain Out-of-School Program (TOSSPro), which was designed to provide an experimental learning program for ten students. Students in TOSSPro participate in learning activities at a nonschool site and in the community. Students at Mark Twain Center who are enrolled in Grades 9, 10, and 11 also have the opportunity to be integrated into special elective courses at Rockville High School. This program provides courses which cannot be offered at Mark Twain because of limited enrollment.

Program Goals

Mark Twain's goal is to help students who are diagnosed emotionally disturbed and who have not been able to attain success in the regular schools to modify inappropriate behaviors, develop academic skills, and return to the mainstream of education. As a result of participation, they will demonstrate a year's growth for each year of instruction in reading and math. The students will also improve their skills in language arts, use of reference materials, and psychomotor skills. The program focuses on the following behavioral/emotional areas: classroom conformity (acceptance of routines and procedures, and classroom persistence with task through management, perseverence), self-worth (presence of self-confidence, personal security, and high self-esteem), self-responsibility (self-evaluation and acceptance of responsibility for success and failure), emotional control (appropriate reaction to tension, frustration, and change), problem solving (active engagement in efforts to cope with and solve problems), acceptance of responsibility (presence of trust and amity in attitudes toward those representing authority), respect for others (acceptance of desirable social standards including rights and property of others), and social skills (acceptance of group standards and ability to work effectively with peers).

A special program is implemented for Mark Twain parents. The parent program is designed to enable parents to understand and take an active role in the development, implementation, and modification of their son's/daughter's individualized educational program.

Major Objectives (Expected Outcomes)

As a result of participation in the Mark Twain Program, it is anticipated that 70 percent of the students who are recommended by the staff to return to the regular Montgomery County Public Schools will attain success in a less restrictive placement, 80 percent of the Mark Twain parents will rate the Mark Twain Program as providing the kind of support and an individualized instruction which meet the needs of their son/daughter, and the staff will receive ongoing training in management of student behavior and development, implementation, and modification of individualized educational programs.

Projected Program Changes (for period through FY 1982)

With the implementation of Public Law 93–142 and reduced state funding of private educational placements for emotionally disturbed students, there has been a significant change in the type of the student placed at Mark

Continued

Illustration No. 12
NEEDS ASSESSMENT

EARLY CHILDHOOD EDUCATION
COMPOSITE RANKINGS

Needs Statements	PTA RANK	PRIN. RANK	TCHR. RANK	BOARD RANK	EXEC. TEAM
1. To provide Early Childhood classes for all five-year-old children in the District born prior to February 1, 1968.	4	1	1	1	
2. To establish Multi-Age Modules (K-1, 2-3) for more effective instruction in the District's elementary schools.					
3. To provide Early Childhood classes for year-old children born prior to who are eligible for sp~ and federal gui~					
4. To					

DALLAS INDEPENDENT SCHOOL DISTRICT
3700 ROSS AVE.

OFFICE MEMO
SCHOOL ADMINISTRATION BUILDING

Operation Involvement Participants

6. TO:	Gerald N. King				
7. FROM:	Priority Ranking of Needs				
8. SUBJECT:	January 12, 1973				
DATE:					

The attached needs statements represent the end of the Needs Assessment phase of the budget preparation cycle. The needs on the attached pages are listed in a composite rank order. This order was obtained by adding up the ranks assigned by each group and assigning the highest priority to the lowest sum. You will note that there was a very high correlation of agreement among the various groups.

Our next responsibility is to translate the identified needs into goals and objectives and propose some possible solutions to the identified needs. As alternative methods for meeting the needs are suggested, these will be planned out to determine if the projected payoff will indeed solve our problems and if it is worth the cost. This phase is scheduled to culminate at our Board of Education Retreat on February 22nd and 23rd.

Needs Statements	PTA	PRIN.	TCHR.	BOARD	EXEC.
9. ~ E					
10. To Ch					
11. To ~ desi~ Effec Pupil~ to Ass		12	10	11	7
12. To con a criter~ learning	9	10	12	12	10
13. To secur~ ...~ reaction with community groups and patrons.	7	13	13	13	12

*Needs Assessment and Priority Ranking of
Needs report to citizen participants from the Dallas Independent School District*

Illustration No. 13

BUDGET PRIORITIES

SCHOOL BOARD LIST OF 1977-78 BUDGET PRIORITIES

As negotiations continue, it may be useful to remember that on Oct. 17, 1977, the Board of Education approved, by unanimous vote, a list of 1977-78 budget priorities, which earlier were endorsed by its finance committee. The SCUSD board action reserves $1.5 million out of a total additional state aid package of $3.7 million. The following is a summary of the board's priorities, as presented to the public on Oct. 17:

PRIORITY	ELEMENTARY	MIDDLE/JR. HIGH	HIGH SCHOOL	TOTAL SCHOOL	CUMULATIVE TOTAL	REMARKS
*1. Classroom Equipment Replacement	$134,247	$58,189	$182,799	$375,235	$375,235	Requests from Equipment Needs Assessment.
**2. Replace Musical Instruments: Maintained by the Instructional Materials Department and allocated based on need.	$30,000	$12,000	$20,000	$62,000	$437,235	Instrumental music has perennially been an integral part of the elementary, middle/jr. high school and high school program of studies. This is an area where pupils have a positive experience that may elude them in some academic areas. For a successful program, instruments must be provided. Through serial numbers, it has been determined that 60% of the 4300 instruments are 25 years or older. A large percentage of the instruments are so old that repair costs are quite high.
**3. Typewriters—High Schools: (40% Implementation of Typewriter Study.)			$165,000	$165,000	$602,235	
*4. Uniform Allowance:			$30,000	$30,000	$632,235	The advent of Title IX requirements has increased participation in girls' competitive activities. This fund would assist student bodies and school budgets in providing uniforms for those related activities. John F. Kennedy would get a one-time allocation of $5,000 because of reduction in the '75–76 school year.
*5. New Equipment	$114,544	$57,266	$121,777	$293,587	$925,822	Requests for new equipment from Needs Assessment.

Note	Elementary	Middle/Jr. High	High School	District	Total
* One Year Expenditures	$438,791	$137,455	$519,570	$310,500	$1,406,322
** Annualized Expenditures	$31,404	$22,486	$54,706	$15,000	$123,596
					$1,529,918

From: Sacramento (CA) Unified School District "newsgram"

Illustration No. 14
BUDGET MESSAGE: PROGRAM QUALITY

In the following paragraphs we will highlight some key features of our school district.

OUTCOMES . . .

Considerable attention has recently been focused on the outcomes of education. We believe that the following are major indicators of quality in the West Chester Area Schools:

National Merit Scholarship Program

During the past four years 91 academically able students from our two high schools have brought considerable honor to our district. Twenty-eight of these students were named Semifinalists in the Merit Program. They scored in the top half of one percent of the nation's graduating senior class. Sixty-three were designated Commended students.

College Board Examination

The Scholastic Aptitude Tests measure students' development in verbal and mathematical reasoning. These tests are predictive measures of the intellectual abilities needed to perform academic tasks well. The SAT measures reasoning abilities that tend to develop slowly over the students' entire life, outside as well as inside the classroom. SAT scores are used to predict students' first-year academic performance in college. While our scores surpass state and national averages, we are concerned about declining scores which have been noted in seven of the last 10 years. Last year 75% of all minority students and 55% of non-minority students took the exams.

College Board Achievement Tests are usually taken by the top third of students who take the College Boards. These tests assess the skills students have developed in a particular subject, their knowledge of the subject, and their ability to apply that knowledge to new materials and situations. Our students score very high on these tests. Our average score in English Composition for last year was 544, compared to a national average of 516. Mathematics scores averaged 578 locally and 547 nationally.

Pennsylvania's Educational Quality Assessment

This testing program is designed to determine how well our schools measure up to Pennsylvania's Ten Goals of Quality Education. While the Goals show academic development as a top priority, they also recognize that habits, feelings and attitudes are not easily separated from knowledge.

Of the 167 scores reported for last year, our schools scored above the expected range 20% of the time, within the range 70% of the time, and below the range 10% of the time. Overall weaknesses were revealed in attitudes toward learning and creative expression. Strengths emerged in health knowledge, appreciation for human achievement and in coping with change.

Noteworthy is the fact that over the past three years verbal scores of our elementary and middle school students rose 4.4% while the state average declined nearly 4%. In the same grades the state mathematics scores dropped over 5% while ours improved by as much as 3.3%. At the high school level our scores declined slightly, but not as much as the state average.

Excerpt from letter dated May 8, 1978 from Dr. Donald E. Langlois, Superintendent to Board of Education and residents reference: 1978 Proposed Budget West Chester Area School District.

Illustration No. 14—(Continued)

Elementary School Achievement Tests

All students in grades one through eight take the Stanford Achievement Tests each spring. Individual tests scores are given to parents, and district results are made public annually. The most recent test results indicate that over 80% of our students are achieving at or above grade level in the basics—reading and mathematics. The results are high in a school system where the average IQ is 108 (high-average).

Dropout Rate

Ten years ago the district's overall dropout rate ws 11.0%. Last year it was 3.4% when 126 students dropped out of school.

The dropout rate for Blacks last year was 5.6%, a significant decline from ten years ago when it was 26.0%.

STAFFING...

For 1978–79, the administration is recommending an average class size of 24 in the elementary schools and 22 in the middle and high schools. Because the anticipated enrollment of 11,128 is 326 fewer pupils than was staffed for this year, and because the unsuccessful alternative school program will be dropped, the teaching staff will be reduced by 22 positions. No other changes in the professional staff are being considered.

In a soon to be released Pennsylvania Economy League report on staffing patterns in 25 large suburban school districts in Southeastern Pennsylvania (excluding Philadelphia), our staffing ratios are as follows:

1977–78 Staffing Ratios per 1,000 Pupils in Twenty-Five Suburban School Districts

	Professional Staff (Teachers, Counselors, Librarians, Administrators)	Non-Professional Staff (Secretarial/Clerial, Aides, Operations/Maintenance)
High	76.1	31.8
Low	57.3	16.2
Average	64.8	22.7
West Chester	61.8	21.3

The average number of years of teaching experience of our teaching staff is 12. Administrators average more than 20 years of professional experience, ten of which are administrative.

Teaching and administrative performance is monitored through a formalized observation and evaluation system. All professional staff are observed and evaluated periodically. During the current year over 2,600 written observations have been recorded, with most being in the "good" to "outstanding" range. Less than 2% of the ratings have been "unsatisfactory."

(Continued on next page)

Program Quality Assessment

Chapter 4

Getting an Overview of the Budget Document

FOR MANY PEOPLE, the single most frightening feature of any school budget is the size of the figures it contains. It seldom deals in the relatively small numbers that are part of our daily family finances. Instead, it generally involves five-and-six-figure sums—sums that seem overwhelming simply by their size. But, in fact, they only *seem* overwhelming. Once you understand how to go about analyzing a budget, the figures it contains will no longer seem so overwhelming. In addition, you should not be intimidated by the professional and technical jargon used in many budgets. They are nothing more than an unfamiliar language. And an unfamiliar language can be learned and mastered.

In this chapter, we are going to propose ways of looking at the budget document and suggest some questions to ask yourself about it. (Later, we will suggest some ways of finding the answers to the questions you'll be asking.) In finding the answers—which may mean finding that in some cases the questions have no answers—you will be discovering a number of important things: whether you're getting the proper value for your educational dollars; whether your district's schools are run efficiently and effectively to meet goals and objectives; whether you and the budget makers share the same educational priorities; whether you and your elected representatives agree about the best ways to finance the schools; whether the budget makers are concealing information from you that you're entitled to have; whether they're misleading you in any way—deliberately or by accident; whether they know how to make up a budget that is comprehensible to citizens, staff and board.

It is not our purpose to set your values for you—to tell you how the schools should be financed or how the money should be divided among various educational programs. These judgments are your prerogatives. Our purpose is to help you find out whether your school budget reflects the judgments you have made.

Getting an overview of the budget. Before trying to analyze, or even to understand, the budget in detail, it is a good idea to have a notion of the document as a whole, even if parts of it still don't make much sense to you (Illustration 15, page 38). Get yourself a copy of the complete budget for the current year, and look it over—if only to get a feel for the kind of material you're going to be working with. You already have an idea, from the material in Chapter 3, of the kind of information a properly-prepared school budget should include; a look through the budget document for your district will give you a sense of how close it comes to that ideal. If you read it with some care—a step which is not necessary at this point, but which you certainly can take if you feel that you are already well enough prepared—you might want to check it against Questions 9 through 15 of the Budget Review Questions (Appendix A). If you can answer "yes" to all of them, you can feel pretty confident that the budget has at least been properly prepared.

Take a look, too, through the proposed and/or tentative budgets, if you have them at hand, as well as any other material the board has prepared for the general public. If they are adequate, you should be able to answer "yes" to Questions 16 and 17 of the Budget Review Questions.

If your look at these documents, whether quick or detailed, indicates that your district's school budget could stand considerable improvement, don't be discouraged. You can, in the future, take steps to bring that improvement about. But before you can do that, you have to understand the budget that you have. So let's get to work with it.

Revenue Items

"How are they spending the money?" may be a far more interesting question than "How much have they got to spend?" But there are good reasons to begin an analysis of the budget figures by looking at the revenue section.

First, and most obvious: it is a simpler place to begin. Although the individual revenue figures are larger than the figures for expenditures, there are fewer of them. That in itself makes them easier to work with.

Moreover, the revenue figures are dollars and cents expressions of a number of important matters of public policy. They reflect a whole series of decisions—by your school board, your community, the state and federal government—about the way to raise and distribute educational funds. For example, are your property taxes high while taxes on business profits are low? Your school board and your state legislature apparently believe that that's a proper arrangement, and their decision is reflected in the revenue figures of your school budget. If you are interested in seeing a reduction in taxes, or the introduction of a new state and local system, there is valuable information for you in the revenue section of your school budget.

Is your school district getting 15% of its revenue from the state while another district is getting 50% or 70%? It was your state legislature that decided on the formula for aid to the various school districts, and if you are interested in changing that formula, you should be interested in the revenue section of the budget. In recent years, this entire issue has become a major concern both of parent/citizen groups and of local school districts and much has already been done to change the system in the direction of greater fairness. Between 1970 and 1978, 22 states took steps to equalize the per-pupil expenditures among their various districts, and in virtually all the remaining states such steps were under consideration, either through discussions in state legislatures or special commissions or as a result of court actions. This same period also saw a change in the source of education money. In the last ten years, largely as a result of decisions by the courts, the percent of school revenues raised from localities, primarily in the form of property taxes, has dropped from 53% to about 48% on a national basis, while the state share has risen from 39% to 44%.

Not only do the revenue figures reflect state policy, they are also a reflection of the way in which your local district operates. They give clues about its efficiency and its openness to the public. It is not uncommon, for example, for budget makers regularly to underestimate school revenue. The practice can serve many purposes: to strengthen the Board's hand if it is engaged in labor negotiations with school employees during budget preparation time; to provide the administration with discretionary funds for unforeseen expenses or for the funding of controversial new positions or programs without public debate; to make possible the reinstatement of employees whose positions were eliminated in economy moves, or to provide a hedge in the event of a last-minute

Illustration No. 15
EXPLANATION OF BUDGET CHANGES

WEST CHESTER AREA SCHOOL DISTRICT
320 North Church Street
WEST CHESTER, PENNSYLVANIA 19380

May 8, 1978

TO: Board of Education and Residents
West Chester Area School District
FROM: Dr. Donald E. Langlois, Superintendent
Rogers W. Vaughn, Chairman
Finance Committee, Board of Education
SUBJECT: 1978-79 Proposed Budget, West Chester Area School District

The proposed 1978-79 budget as presented here is $24,892,500—an increase of $1,643,800 or 7.1% over the current year's estimated expenditure of $23,248,700. This budget would result in a 2.0 mil tax decrease (2.4%) for Chester County residents and a 0.4 mill tax decrease (0.2%) for Delaware County residents. Reasons for this favorable impact on taxes despite a 7.1% increase in expenses are:

- A projected balance of $966,800 from this year's operations. (Expenses are under budget by $622,900 and income is expected to exceed budget by $343,900. The expenses are down for a number of reasons: the non-retirement of the High Street property debt, non-filling of budgeted instructional positions due to lower than anticipated enrollments, and a close observance of all operations to ensure the need for expenditures. Income exceeds budget because: the increase in state subsidy occurred after this year's tax rate was set, we experienced increased earnings from investments, and there was an increase in real estate transfer taxes.)

- A $184,000 (3.8%) increase in state reimbursement.

- A 3.1% tax base increase in Chester County and 0.9% in Delaware County.

The total salary and wage expense is budgeted at $14,608,500—a 5.6% increase over the current year. Employee benefits, including those mandated by law as well as those negotiated on a local basis, are budgeted at $2,445,000 or a 13.8% increase. These two items account for 68.5% of the proposed budget. A major new cost of $113,800 in the benefit area is the result of mandated unemployment compensation insurance. Anticipated rate increases are 4% for Blue Cross/Blue Shield, 10% for dental insurance, and 10% for prescription drug insurance.

Transportation costs continue to increase sharply as services are expanded for nonpublic school children.

change in state or federal appropriations. Most school districts have loose controls over their actual expenditures during any given year; if revenues are underestimated, individual items can be overspent and generally no one will know about it—or, revenues may be underestimated as a way of making the official look good when he concludes that the district has more money than it thought; to test community reaction to a possible tax increase; to offset an anticipated recession or cut in taxes or state aid. And there is always the possibility of inefficiency and incompetence, unchecked from year to year, that regularly produces an underestimation of school revenue.

If the budget document in your school district is reasonably well prepared, the current budget will include comparative figures for previous years. So an examination of its revenue section will tell you several important things and, at the same time, probably raise some equally important questions.

After reading through it, you should know, for example:

- How much of the district's revenue is raised through local taxes.

- How much the state provides—either through the state foundation grant or the state aid formula.

- How much the state provides for so-called categorical (specifically designated) programs.

- How much the federal government provides, both for general and categorical purposes.

And questions like these may occur to you (later on we will discuss ways of finding out their answers. Here we want only to indicate the kinds of questions you may want to look into):

- Do any additional possible sources of revenue exist other than the ones listed in the budget? (Such sources could include taxes on wages or income; occupancy taxes; taxes on business goods; sales taxes; per capita taxes.)

- Has the amount of the local property tax revenue in your school budget changed in the last few years? If so, why? Was it a change in the tax rate, the assessment rate, the market value of the real estate in your community? How does the change compare to the rate of inflation?

- If yours is a growing community, does the current revenue figure reflect the anticipated increase in real estate values—and, therefore, the basis on which property taxes are computed?

- Similarly, if your community raises a portion of its school revenue through a tax on wages or income, does the current budget take into account an anticipated rise in these figures?

- How accurately have the budget makers anticipated the state and federal contributions to your district?

- Has there been any persistent pattern of misestimation of revenue items in your district's budget?

Expenditure Items

The expenditure section is the part of the budget that most directly reflects the district's educational plans and priorities and its efficiency of operation. Whether your main concern is with the educational program in general or with a specific educational program, whether it is with educational costs in general or with the costs in a specific area of the school budget, the expenditures section is the place to look for what you want to know.

Not that you're likely to be able to find it easily. It is more than 20 years since program budgeting—allocating expenditures to the programs they are designed to serve—was first adopted by a number of public agencies. Even so, the majority of school districts still use the old line item format—not only in their dealings with the state, where it may be required, but in their dealings with their communities. And the line item format, which categorizes budget items by the function they serve rather than the educational activity they represent, makes it difficult to get accurate information about the amount of money involved in any given educational program. The line item budget probably will contain no entry for the third grade reading program, for example. Instead, the program's costs will be apportioned among such functional categories as "Administration," "Instruction," "Pupil Personnel Service," "Operations and Maintenance''—categories which are themselves further sub-divided into "salaries," "materials and supplies," "contracted services," etc.

Even so, a line item budget can tell you a number of important things about educational programs in your community. Once you know how to analyze it, you'll be able to investigate such questions as these:

Which items—whether line or program—have been increased (or decreased) from one year to the next, and why? Many school districts prepare their budgets on an "incremental" basis, simply taking it for granted that the programs and expenditures of the current and past year will continue into next year—with some slight increase to cover inflation, or some other minor change to deal with a shift in educational emphasis. Rarely do the budget makers explicitly examine the goals of the school's district, or alternative approaches to teaching or learning; and very rarely do they drop positions or programs. But "We've always done things that way" is hardly a reason for continuing the practice, and parents/citizens who have made a comparative study of budget expenditures can take steps to bring about the changes they think are necessary.

Another favorite argument that the budget makers advance to justify particular increases or decreases is that the state requires the board to spend certain sums of money in certain specific ways. "Only 15% (or 20%, or whatever) is discretionary, the rest is mandated," is a common response to questions about specific expenditures for specific budget items. But the fact is that although specific programs and services indeed may be mandated by the state, it is up to the school district to determine the way these mandates will be met. The state may require four years of high school English, but it is up to the district to decide whether to fulfill that requirement with courses in Remedial English, Advanced Placement English, Business English, College Preparatory English or a single minimum competency English course each year. If the state requires transportation for students living beyond a certain number of miles from the school (and reimburses the district for some of the expenditures involved), it is up to the district to decide whether to buy buses, or lease them, or contract transportation to an outside company, or to make some arrangement with the community's mass transit system. Citizens should also have in hand a copy of the state codes to see for themselves what the state actually requires.

Are any increases or decreases in specific items out of line with the increases or decreases in others—do any changes in allocations stand out like sore thumbs? If, for example, the overall budget has been increased by 7% while the kindergarten program was increased by only 2%, you'll probably want to know the reasons. You'll probably want to look into the reasons, too, if you find that a 6% increase has been budgeted for some salaries while the district's special education program is still underfunded. Nor should you permit yourself to fall into the trap of trading off educational programs when you see that funding for one has been disproportionately decreased or when you find that the one you're particularly interested in is not getting as much money as you'd like. There's no reason to look for funds by reducing other academic or student-oriented services if there is a chance of finding the necessary money elsewhere.

Have the budget makers in the past accurately estimated the expenditure portion of the budget and, if they haven't, which sections have they estimated accurately? In some school districts, expenditures in certain categories are regularly overestimated in order to suggest to the board that larger allocations will be needed for the forthcoming year. In other instances, board members may direct administrators to estimate current teachers' salaries at a high level so that the figure proposed for the next year's budget will appear low and the board will be able to conduct its salary negotiations with the teachers without letting the union know just how much more the proposed budget has actually provided for their salaries. And don't be put off by people who tell you not to bother looking at the salary items, since usually they are all negotiated by collective bargaining. Aside from everything else, the funds allocated to salaries and benefits often make up 70% to 80% of the total budget and if the upcoming year's union contracts have not yet been negotiated when you start your budget study, you *can* influence the amount allocated for salaries by the kinds of changes you propose. For example, attrition (resignations and retirements), can reduce the number of maintenance personnel and, therefore, the overall expenses for maintenance; reduction in the student/teacher ratio may increase the total amount spent on teachers' salaries. The "fixed charges" section is another one you should examine, even though this section, too, is likely to be described as one you can do nothing about. Many of the items in this section relate to employee benefits, which can be altered by union negotiations or by the total number of employees. Others, like payroll taxes, although fixed by the government, vary depending on the total amount allocated for salaries.

Do the figures that are budgeted have any real meaning in your district? Although one of the functions of the budget is to control expenditures in advance, school budgets are never looked at as straitjackets, and in some districts, the amounts budgeted and those that are actually spent bear only the faintest resemblance to one another. Moreover, most states permit budgetary transfers and modifications that enable district superintendents to change the amounts allocated to individual items by transferring funds among the various budget categories. Most states require the school board to approve such transfers and a few require that when changes are made, the amended budget be submitted to the state department of education. But the community as a whole is seldom informed about the matter and parents/citizens almost never participate in the decision to transfer funds. If you find significant discrepancies repeated over a period of time between the actual expenditures in your school district and the figures it proposes in its budget, you can be pretty sure you're dealing with a school board and a district administration that treat the budget as their private preserve.

How do educational expenses in your district compare with those in other parts of the state and with the nation as a whole? Clearly, this is an important question for investigation. If your district—or your state—is short-changing students in any way, you surely want to know about it. And even if your district is spending an adequate amount per pupil on educational services, there are other comparative figures you will want to look into—salaries, fringe benefits, class size, student/teacher ratios, employee sick days, sabbatical policies, policies regarding teacher preparation time and travel allowances—a detailed list of costs that affect, directly or indirectly, the quality of education in your district.

Chapter 5
The Budget Process

EQUALLY AS IMPORTANT as the budget is the process by which it is hammered out—the process that determines what the content of that budget will be. If you are to have any impact on that content, you have to be familiar with the budget process and know how to work with and through it to make your influence felt.

You may not find it easy. The budget processes in local school districts are as varied as the budgets they produce. Although most states set forth a number of minimal requirements and regulations governing the budget process (Illustrations 18 and 19, pages 51 and 52)—regulations and requirements that also vary in their specific forms from state to state—these regulations are not always adhered to. In some communities, the budget process is orderly and open—not only leaving room for active citizen participation, but actually encouraging it. But in others, the public has virtually no idea of what the process is, and is, in fact, discouraged from participating in it—whether because the board and the administration want to keep control in their own hands or because the budget process is so disorganized and haphazard it is almost impossible to find out what is actually going on. In some small communities, for example, there may be no formal guidelines whatever and the whole matter may be left in the hands of the superintendent, who issues his instructions in a series of memos to his staff; these memos constitute the only written information available on the way budget planning and preparation are carried out. Even worse, he may issue his instructions verbally, in which case parents/citizens have absolutely nothing to go on.

Fortunately, however, some districts *do* prepare Budget Calendars, more or less detailed, which describe the tasks involved in budget preparation, the participants in those tasks, and the dates on which each task is to be completed. Although such calendars are not themselves descriptions of the budget process, they do offer at least an outline of the steps that are taken inside the school administration in preparation for drawing up the budget (Illustrations 17 and 19, pages 50 and 52).

Most of the items on the Calendar refer to what we call the Internal Budget Process—the preparatory work and analysis performed by the professional staff and presented to the superintendent—and, in some cases, the board—as a basis on which to draw up the Proposed Budget for the coming year (Illustration 18, page 51). In a community where the budget process as a whole is open and orderly, the information that emerges from the various stages of this internal process will be made available to parents/citizens, so that they can use it in connection with their own budget studies and budget evaluation and can function effectively in the External Budget Process—the stages in the development of the Budget that directly call for public participation. Public hearings, for example, are part of the *external* process, and the public's input at those hearings should weigh heavily with both the board and the superintendent.

Since the budget process varies so sharply from one community to another, we cannot give you a description of it that is guaranteed to fit the situation in your community. We can, however, indicate the way the process *should* work if it is to be orderly and open—if it is to leave ample room for public participation and if it is to be organized in such a way as to assure adequate feedback, at every step, which will then be taken into consideration as the process continues on to the next step.

And now to the list. As you'll see, we have translated into plain English the professional jargon in which the budget process is too often described. And we have also indicated the extent of the role that parents/citizens should play in every step along the way.

The Basic Steps in the Budget Process

1 . **Establish objectives:** Decide what it is we want to have happen to the kids in our schools—in every classroom, in every school building, and in the district as a whole. (This is a process that should be carried out by the entire community—not merely by the board and the district administration, but also by concerned parents/citizens.)

2. **Take stock:** Determine what *is* happening at all these levels now. (School professionals are in the best position to carry through this study, but their findings should be made available to the whole community.)

3. **Clarify needs:** Compare what is happening with what we want to have happen. (Like step 1, this is a process in which parents/citizens, as well as board and administration, should play a part.)

4. **Identify priorities:** Decide the order of importance of the various things we want, at the classroom, school, and district levels. (Here, too, parents/citizens should be actively involved.)

5. **Specify alternative programs and services to meet the needs:** Spell out a number of different ways of satisfying the needs and priorities that have been determined, and establish standards for judging them. (This is a task for school professionals, whose findings should be reported to the whole community.)

6. **Cost out the programs:** Attach a price tag to every program and service, specifying the level and standard each of the amounts would satisfy. (A task for the district administration, with findings to be reported to the community.)

7. **Evaluate current programs, services, and activities:** Examine current services, programs, and activities to determine whether they are meeting the objectives that have been set, and if they are not, the changes that are needed to bring them into line. This step also provides information for establishing new objectives. (A task for the community as well as for the board and the professionals.)

8. **Build preliminary program format:** Decide on the programs and services to be offered during the coming year, based on the information that emerged from steps 3, 5, and 7. (Like step 6, a task for the district administration, reporting to the community.)

9. **Identify and cost out central support services needed:** Determine what will be needed—in administrative personnel, maintenance, transportation and food services—to support the schools' programs and how much these supports will cost. (Carried out by the

Illustration No. 16
INSTRUCTIONS FOR SCHOOL BUDGET

SCHOOL DISTRICT BUDGETS

I. LEGAL REQUIREMENTS

Section 17-1, *The School Code of Illinois*, requires that the board of education of each school district under 500,000 inhabitants shall adopt an annual budget within or before the first quarter of each fiscal year. School districts governed by a board of directors are not legally required to adopt a budget, but the expenditures shall be approved in advance by the Superintendent, Educational Service Region. However, it is recommended that such districts develop a budget to aid in the planning of educational programs and to provide sound fiscal controls.

II. PROCEDURE FOR PREPARATION AND ADOPTION OF BUDGET

Establish a Fiscal Year—The board of education shall establish a fiscal year for the school district—(Section 17-1). It is common practice to establish July 1 of one year through June 30 of the following year as the fiscal year.

Designate a Person or Persons to Prepare a Tentative Budget—The board of education, by resolution, shall designate some person or persons to prepare a tentative budget. A suggested resolution follows:

BE IT RESOLVED by the Board of Education of School District Number _____ in the County of _____, State of Illinois, that _____ is hereby appointed to prepare a tentative budget for said School District for the fiscal year beginning _____, 19_____, and ending _____, 19_____, which tentative budget shall be filed with the Secretary of this Board.

Prepare a Budget in Tentative Form—The person or persons designated to prepare the tentative budget may use Form IOE 50-06, which was prepared to meet requirements of *The School Code of Illinois* and to provide a standard budget format for all districts. Certain districts may need more detail than is provided on the Form. In this case, a summary work schedule may be prepared and maintained as a part of the district's records. The budget may also be expanded to include more detail utilizing the Chart of Accounts provided in the *Illinois Financial Accounting Manual for Local School Systems, Circular Series A, Number 246* (Revised January 1972).

Make the Tentative Budget Available to Public Inspection—The Secretary of the Board of Education shall make the tentative budget available for public inspection at least 30 days prior to final action.

Hold at Least One Public Hearing—The board of education shall hold at least one public hearing on the proposed budget prior to final action. A notice stating the location, date, and hour of the public hearing shall be placed in a newspaper published in such district, at least 30 days prior to the time of the hearing. If there should not be a newspaper published in such district, notices of the public hearing shall be posted thereof in five of the most public places of such district. Notices of the public hearing, whether published or posted, should read substantially as follows:

State of Illinois, Illinois Office of Education "Instructions for School District Budgeting."

district administration; findings reported to the community.)

10. **Build preliminary expenditures budget:** This document is based on the information coming out of steps 6, 8, and 9, and determines next year's costs. (To be carried through by school professionals, with findings made available to the whole community.)

Illustration No. 16—(*Continued*)

NOTICE OF PUBLIC HEARING

NOTICE IS HEREBY GIVEN by the Board of Education of School District Number ____, in the County of _____, State of Illinois, that tentative budget for said School District for the fiscal year beginning _____, 19____, will be on file and conveniently available to public inspection at _____

Address

_____, Illinois in this School District from and after _____o'clock _____m.,

City

on the _____ day of _____, 19____. Notice is further hereby given that a public hearing on said budget will be held at _____o'clock _____m., on the _____ day of _____, 19____, at _____ in this School District Number _____. Dated this _____ day of _____ 19____. Board of Education of School District Number_____, in the County of _____, State of Illinois.

By_____

Secretary

Make any Necessary Changes in the Budget—If, as a result of the public hearing, it should be determined that certain changes in the budget are necessary, these changes should be made before the budget is adopted.

Adopt the Budget—The budget shall be adopted prior to making the tax levy if the beginning of the fiscal year should be subsequent to the time that the tax levy shall be made for such fiscal year. The adoption of the budget shall be by roll call vote and the resolution adopting the budget shall be incorporated into the official minutes of the meeting of the board of education. The resolution adopting the budget shall be in the following form:

ADOPTION OF BUDGET

The Budget shall be approved and signed by members of the School Board as illustrated below:

Adopted this _____ day of _____, 19____, by a roll call vote of _____ Yeas, and _____ Nays, to wit:

Members Voting Yea:	Members Voting Nay:
_____	_____
_____	_____
_____	_____
_____	_____
_____	_____
_____	_____

Notice of Public Hearing

11. **Review preliminary estimates of anticipated revenue:** Estimate how much money will be coming into the school district next year and examine possible sources of additional revenue. (To be carried out in the same way as step 10.)

Illustration No. 17
SCHEDULE FOR BUDGET DEVELOPMENT

SAN FRANCISCO UNIFIED SCHOOL DISTRICT
SCHEDULE FOR DEVELOPMENT OF
FISCAL YEAR 1979 BUDGET

NO.	ACTIVITY	STARTING DATE	COMPLETION DATE
21.	Program budget printout returned to Budget & Finance Department; Budget & Finance Department checks for accuracy; modifications are made, if necessary, additional printouts are produced	12/13/77	12/13/77
22.	County General Education Fund budgets approved by Board of Education and forwarded to Budget Division of the Controller's Office	—	1/10/78
23.	Budget development materials and per pupil allocations distributed to site principals; principals develop plans for distribution of funds	1/6/78	1/27/78
24.	Preliminary Budget Report is prepared and distributed to Superintendent, Board of Education, schools, organizations and community	12/14/77	12/20/77
25.	Legal deadline for notifying principals of possible release from positions for the 1978–79 school year (Education Code Section 44951)	—	3/1/78
26.	Legal deadline for notifying all certificated employees, other than principals, of possible release from positions for the 1978–79 school year. (Education Code Section 44949)	—	3/15/78
27.	Budget requests reviewed by Task Force with Budget Managers and Program Managers; modifications coded and programmed; report is prepared and submitted to Superintendent, Board of Education, schools, organizations and community	1/5/78	3/3/78
28.	Budget and Finance Committee of Board of Education begins weekly meetings to review and analyze budget and to receive input from community and staff	1/3/78	3/7/78

An Excerpt for the SCHEDULE FOR DEVELOPMENT OF FISCAL 1979 BUDGET San Francisco Unified School District, 1977, Page 4 of 7 pages.

12. **Set priority needs on a district-wide basis:** Compare what the community wants for the entire district with the needs of its individual schools and with the school superintendent's assessment of the district-wide needs. (Here there should be full participation by the community, the board and the professionals.)

Illustration No. 18
BUDGET PREPARATION PROCESS

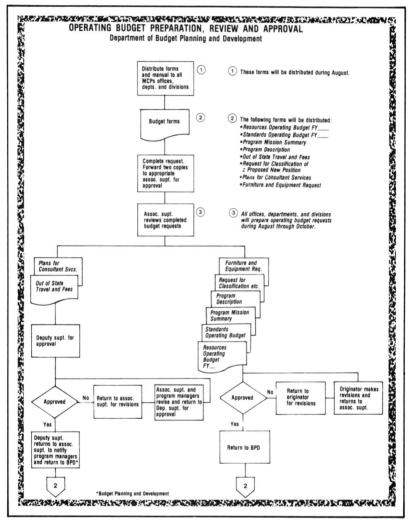

OPERATING BUDGET PREPARATION, REVIEW AND APPROVAL
Department of Budget Planning and Development

Distribute forms and manual to all MCPs offices, depts. and divisions ① — ① These forms will be distributed during August.

Budget forms ② — ② The following forms will be distributed:
• *Resources Operating Budget FY____*
• *Standards Operating Budget FY____*
• *Program Mission Summary*
• *Program Description*
• *Out of State Travel and Fees*
• *Request for Classification of a Proposed New Position*
• *Plans for Consultant Services*
• *Furniture and Equipment Request*

Complete request. Forward two copies to appropriate assoc. supt. for approval

Assoc. supt. reviews completed budget requests ③ — ③ All offices, departments, and divisions will prepare operating budget requests during August through October.

Plans for Consultant Svcs.

Out of State Travel and Fees

Furniture and Equipment Req.

Request for Classification etc.

Program Description

Program Mission Summary

Standards Operating Budget

Resources Operating Budget FY__

Deputy supt. for approval

Approved — No → Return to assoc. supt. for revisions — Assoc. supt. and program managers revise and return to Dep. supt. for approval

Approved — No → Return to originator for revisions — Originator makes revisions and returns to assoc. supt.

Yes

Yes

Deputy supt. returns to assoc. supt. to notify program managers and return to BPD*

Return to BPD

*Budget Planning and Development

2

2

Excerpt from Budget Preparation, Review and Approval Chart.
Montgomery County (MD) Public Schools FY 1981, *Illustration of "internal process."*

Illustration No. 19
BUDGET DEVELOPMENT SCHEDULE

PROPOSED PROGRAM BUDGET DEVELOPMENT SCHEDULE

The following dates are submitted for scheduling purposes. They are established with the intent of completing the 1976-77 Program Budget not later than June 30, 1976.

Date	Activity
Needs Assessment Phase	
September—October—November, 1975	Conduct Needs Assessment (Staff Members will study and correlate recommendations of Skyline Wide Educational Plan, Chase Report, Task Force For Educational Excellence, Research and Evaluation Reports)
December, 1975	Staff Analyzes results of Needs Assessment Survey
January 14, 15, 21, 1976	Results of Needs Assessment Presented To Board Committees
February 4, 1976	Committee of the Whole meets to give final guidance to Program Managers regarding priority program thrusts for 1976-77. (Operation Involvement representatives will be invited to attend)
Program Planning Phase	
February, March, April, 1976	Program managers prepare Program Budgets
May 6, 12, 19, 1976	Program Managers present Program Budgets to Board Committees for review.
Approval Phase	
June 2, 1976	Committee of Whole reviews Program Budgets and gives final guidance (Fine Tuning). (Operation Involvement Representatives will be invited to attend).
June 16, 1976	Special Meeting of Board of Education for public hearing of proposed budget.
June 23, 1976 (Board Meeting)	Approve 1976-77 Budget and set tax rate.

"Budget Development Schedule" Dallas, Texas Independent School District

13. **Build and present proposed budget, with superintendent's message:** Spell out on paper the budget objectives, program costs and revenues, identifying programs and/or services that have been added or dropped and explaining the reasons for these changes. (Like step 10—a job for the professionals, reporting to the community as a whole.)

14. **Board review of the superintendent's proposed budget:** Determine the areas in which the board agrees and disagrees with the budget proposed by the superintendent. (This step involves a board meeting at which parents/citizens should be present as observers.)

15. **Public hearings:** Board and administration explain to the community the differences that may exist among the findings of the needs assessment, the superintendent's proposed budget and the board's assessment. Community members offer testimony on desired changes in the budget. (Obviously, this step involves extensive efforts to get full community participation.)

16. **Modification and board adoption of tentative budget:** Based on the outcome of the public hearing, the board makes the changes it deems necessary in the proposed budget and adopts it as a tentative budget. (Parents/citizens should be present as observers at this board meeting, also.)

17. **Review tentative budget at building levels:** Determine at open meetings what the tentative budget will mean for each individual school district. (Obviously, this is a place for full and direct community participation.)

18. **Review tentative budget at district-wide meetings:** Determine at open meetings what the tentative budget means for the district as a whole. (Again, full and direct community participation.)

19. **Announce superintendent's recommendations to modify tentative budget:** Superintendent proposes which of the suggestions made at the school building and district-wide meetings should be incorporated into the final budget. (The superintendent's recommendations should be made available to every member of the community.)

20. **Public hearing:** Citizens—as individuals and as groups—inform the board of items they want included in—or left out of—the tentative budget. (Obviously, this calls for full community participation.)

21. **Board adoption of final budget:** After reviewing the changes proposed by the superintendent and the public, the board revises the budget, if necessary, and the adopts it in its final form. (Citizens

should sit in as observers at the board meeting where this takes place.)

This is what an orderly and open budget process would be like. One final step, however, is necessary in communities that are not fiscally independent, and must submit their budgets for approval to an outside agency:

22. **Budget submitted to funding body or voters:** Board and administration gather public support for their budget and present it for approval if they live in a fiscally dependent school district or in a community required to hold a tax levy referendum. If the budget is reduced or approval is not granted, steps 18, 19, 20 and 21 should be repeated.

*　　　*　　　*　　　*　　　*　　　*　　　*

The steps in the budget process that we have spelled out here make the whole process sound simpler and more direct than it is likely to be in even the best organized and most open school district. Steps that appear quite easy to perform when they're described in the general terms we have used are, in reality, complicated, involving any number of sub-steps and detailed analyses. The four words of step 6—"Cost out the programs"—may require the skills of a large number of people, putting in hundreds of hours of work.

The list cannot tell you which steps in the budget preparation process in your community are the crucial ones—the ones at which the most important decisions are made. In the ideal budget process we have outlined here, the public hearings play an important part. But if yours is a community in which the public meetings are no more than window dressing, the important decisions are likely to be made entirely behind the scenes. So it is important for you to become familiar with the internal process in your community: only that way will you be able to discover the stages that represent genuine turning points in the development of the budget. Later we will suggest ways to find out—to the degree your community makes it possible—about the internal and external budget processes. Here we want merely to suggest to you what a budget process should be, so that when you get down to the business of finding out about that process in your community, you will have a reasonably good idea of the kinds of things to look for.

A Look at the Internal Budget Process: Different Approaches to the Same End

The early 1960's saw the introduction into the school budget preparation process in some districts of the **Program, Planning, Budget System (PPBS)**—a system adopted from the one used in the U.S. Defense Department by Robert McNamara, then Secretary of Defense. Budgets prepared according to this system showed more than costs and revenues. They defined program goals for the district and showed the way the budget figures were connected with the planned objectives.

The PPBS budget was followed by the simpler system of program budgeting. As we have said, program budgeting has not yet been adopted by all states or all school districts (California, Colorado, and Oregon use it). It remains a goal toward which many concerned citizens are pressing.

But even after the push for program budgeting got under way, a new budget preparation process arrived on the scene. The main attraction of this system, called **Zero Based Budgeting**, lay in its promise—in an era of declining school enrollment and taxpayer revolt—to put more effective controls on the school budget than had ever been exerted before.

In essence, Zero Based Budgeting is a system that requires justifying every expenditure in the budget from point zero. It calls on the budget makers to ask what would happen if the individual items or programs in the budget were to receive no funds at all. In ZBB, the budget is broken down into decision packages, each of which then receives a priority rating by successively higher levels of administration. The decision packages, each of which describes a specific type of program activity, can show different ways of performing the same function, or they can cost out programs at different levels, each starting at point zero.

As the packages are presented to the various levels of school management—the package on remedial reading, for example, starting with the Remedial Reading Director, moving to the Director of the

Language Arts Program, then on to the Assistant Superintendent for Curriculum, then the superintendent, and finally to the school board—they are ranked, in order of their decreasing benefit to the schools, in terms of resources, price tags, consequences, intended accomplishments, and the alternatives in the same field. With each package now rated according to its level of benefit, it can be determined which programs to fund. Obviously, those that receive money will be those that have been rated at or above the level of benefit that has been adopted as a minimum.

A modification of ZBB has been used successfully in the Greece, New York, Central School District, where there was a long history of citizen rejection of the school budgets proposed by the board. In Greece, the budget alternatives did not start from a zero base. Instead, the base was one that provided only the minimum school services required by law, and budgets were then calculated first on an austerity level and then at the level of "business as usual." In building the 150 decision packages from which the budget was finally chosen, there was considerable comment and suggestion from the entire community—school personnel (from maintenance to administrative), parents, and citizens. In making its decision about which programs to fund, the board played off cost/benefits in each package, so that it could provide, as D. Robinson wrote in the September 1976 issue of *Educational Economics*, "the most it feels it can get for the money it has to spend."

Still another approach to budget preparation is **Multi-Level Standards Based Budgeting**, a process adopted by the Montgomery County, Maryland, Board of Education. Here, too, the community is involved in the budget preparation process, particularly in determining the educational priorities the budget is designed to meet. Priorities are established by the board after gathering information at a number of public meetings. Then three different kinds of budgets are spelled out, each at a different level of spending—the first, the same as the level currently in effect; the second, the current level plus expected increases due to inflation; the third, the level required to produce improved or expanded services. At each spending level, the budget must describe the standards it will meet in connection with resources (personnel and/or the services they perform);

services (the programs or activities—how often and how many pupils they serve); and outcomes (the result that the services and resources are expected to achieve).

And finally, there is the process which combines **Management By Objectives,** program budgeting and project management. It is used by the Dallas Independent School District. Here the budget makers, after examining the current level of services, assessing educational needs and determining and costing out educational goals, examine each goal in terms of its payoff and rank each one "according to its worth and cost in competition with all other goals," as the Dallas School District writes in its description of the process.

Getting to Work—
What You Will Need to Get Started

IF YOU ARE TO BE able to study and work with the budget effectively, you will need a number of documents, both from your local school district and from your state department of education (or, as it may be called, department of public instruction.) All of them are open to public inspection and you should be able to get them simply by a letter or visit to the appropriate agency, but you may be charged for copies so inquire about this. (Later in this chapter, you will find sample letters as well as suggestions for other steps to take if a letter is not the best approach or if, for some reason, it produces no response.) Don't be discouraged if you can't immediately get hold of all of them. As long as you have your district's budget for the current year and its actual income and expenditure figures for the preceding year, you have the documents you need to make a start.

Materials From Your School District

The list below looks longer than it actually is. You may well find that nearly all the items on it are included in the very first one. (In addition, a few other documents are needed to study the budget *process* as well as the budget. These are listed on page 66.)

1 . The Current Year's Budget—not a summary, but the *complete* budget as it was adopted by the school board before the start of the year.

2. The Proposed and/or Tentative Budgets for the coming year. If you start your budget study early enough in the fiscal year, these documents may not yet be available.

3. The Popularized Budget for the current year.

4. The Complete School Budgets for the two preceding years.

5. The Actual Income and Expenditure Record for the two past years (await end-of-the-year report). If these figures are not included in the current year's budget, they can be obtained from your state education department: most states require that all school districts file an annual financial report with this agency. Or ask your district office for a copy of its annual audit report. The format may differ from the annual budget but the categories of income and expenditure are usually the same as the Chart of Accounts.

6. The Actual Income and Expenditures for the current year, up to the most recent month. This information is often distributed at school board meetings and is a part of the board minutes.

7. The Estimated Income and Expenditures through the end of the current year. This material may be available in a separate document or it may form part of the proposed budget for the coming year.

8. The district's Educational Plan

9. The district's Long-Range Plan

10. The district's Needs Assessments for the current and previous two years—if there is one.

11. The district's Educational and Budget Priorities. These—if they exist—may be in the form of a single list, or they may appear in separate lists drawn up by the various groups involved in establishing priorities: the superintendent, the board, the teachers, the students, the Citizens' Advisory Committee and/or any other groups concerned with the schools.

12. Budget Policies. Every district has a statement of policies, adopted by the board, that indicates the way responsibility for educational matters is divided, the ways tax moneys are to be used, etc.

13. Budget Guidelines. These should include information about such items as textbooks, staff-to-pupil ratios, expenditures per pupil, etc. (Illustration 8, pages 22 and 23).

Material from the State Department of Education

Although this list is shorter than the one above, you may have to do a little more work to get the documents it calls for. You should write separate letters of request for each one of them, since each will probably have to go to a separate office to be filled (you may want to send requests by certified mail). Most state education departments respond fairly quickly to requests for single pieces of information, but a letter that contains more than one request is likely to be answered only after a long time or only incompletely. It is the easiest thing in the world for it to be lost in the shuffle as it moves from one office to another.

1. The form on which all school districts are required to report their budgets to the state.

2. Annual Financial Statistical Report on Revenue and Expenditures. In most states, this document lists each school district's per-pupil expenditures for various categories of items (see illustration 20). In a few states, however, it lists only the expenditure categories and the totals spent in each. If yours is such a state, you will have to make an additional request: for the figure representing the average daily attendance (ADA) in each district. Once you have the ADA figures, you can find the per-pupil expenditures yourself, by dividing the ADA figures into the figure representing expenditures. If yours is one of the very few states in which funding is based on enrollment or average daily membership (ADM) you will need the ADM figures.

3. Description of the State Program for Financial Support to the Schools—or, if your state does not have such a document, a written explanation of the formula used to determine grants to school districts. This would include information not only on policies related to general education, but also to such special categories as vocational-technical education, programs for the disadvantaged, special education, etc.

4. The Chart of Accounts (Illustration 21, page 63). The state accounting system sends every school district a copy of this document, which lists the budget and accounting code numbers that are

Illustration No. 20

COMPARATIVE PER PUPIL EXPENDITURE

TABLE 4

EXPENDITURES PER AVERAGE DAILY MEMBERSHIP FOR SELECTED FUNCTIONS BY COUNTY AND SCHOOL DISTRICTS 1976-77

SCHOOL DISTRICTS	ADMINISTRATION $	INSTRUCTION $	PUPIL PERS SERVICES $	OP & MAINT OF PLANT $	FIXED CHARGES $	TRANSPORTATION $	OTHERS $	CURRENT EXPEND $	RANK	TOTAL EXPEND $	RANK
COUNTY	62.17	782.74	30.03	171.75	135.37	74.18	51.36	1,307.61		1,533.91	
BEDFORD											
BEDFORD AREA S D	47.60	770.49	16.25	146.01	127.32	89.93	25.91	1,223.50	370	1,254.05	484
CHESTNUT RIDGE S D	62.47	703.65	23.64	199.67	122.33	158.72	41.24	1,311.71	250	1,438.59	324
EVERETT AREA S D	70.19	705.02	18.65	162.13	133.77	137.21	62.19	1,289.16	280	1,363.59	411
NORTHN BEDFORD CO. S D	51.54	791.04	16.65	153.94	110.60	100.60	41.20	1,291.09	278	1,416.74	346
TUSSEY MOUNTAIN S D	60.06	791.76	18.75	157.90	119.72	140.97	44.14	1,333.29	229	1,370.69	282
COUNTY	57.86	746.14	18.96	162.43	130.76	122.57	42.13	1,280.87		1,370.69	
BERKS											
ANTIETAM S D	86.99	899.39	25.42	201.56	155.20	31.69	45.21	1,445.48	140	1,816.34	67
BOYERTOWN AREA S D	47.83	850.21	45.95	156.73	106.85	16.63	30.39	1,367.71	193	1,639.52	144
BRANDYWINE HGTS AREA S D	53.64	687.65	26.47	159.91	123.35	66.32	37.68	1,136.42	359	1,385.36	485
CONRAD WEISER A S D	71.57	786.48	29.19	137.27	132.95	62.14	19.92	1,229.26	249	1,469.57	289
DANIEL BOONE AREA S D	60.64	796.24	36.41	146.24	129.93	108.19	32.84	1,313.61	341	1,436.40	327
EXETER TOWNSHIP S D	61.93	789.68	30.70	157.60	125.84	51.47	35.45	1,247.02	247	1,509.28	258
FLEETWOOD AREA S D	69.80	897.35	31.50	167.06	178.21	54.50	41.70	1,313.80	253	1,625.60	153
GOVERNOR MIFFLIN S D	56.43	775.50	23.18	202.01	140.21	72.02	39.82	1,279.82	298	1,625.60	257
HAMBURG AREA S D	53.41	775.51	29.34	167.91	140.80	48.00	29.84	1,277.87	296	1,682.80	257
KUTZTOWN AREA S D	64.51	775.51	33.44	146.94	138.45	93.28	29.84	1,277.87	296	1,509.78	53
MUHLENBERG TWP S D	65.59	897.68	33.44	247.96	170.08	48.00	19.55	1,509.46	363	1,864.88	396
OLEY VALLEY S D	63.51	788.47	33.36	172.52	132.38	75.84	51.00	1,226.17	158	1,374.88	163
READING S D	41.01	874.52	33.36	174.76	177.10	17.80	59.00	1,428.08	159	1,612.84	53
SCHUYLKILL VALLEY S D	59.29	853.04	20.59	143.71	144.25	103.51	28.08	1,082.99	491	1,273.33	472
TULPEHOCKEN AREA S D	55.10	665.67	9.26	163.82	99.40	81.77	28.08	1,082.99	491	1,283.80	138
TWIN VALLEY S D	55.42	906.60	28.00	204.61	155.14	17.44	42.30	1,488.71	106	1,650.07	169
WILSON S D	58.88	680.99	34.04	200.00	149.41	40.36	37.45	1,351.66	209	1,599.85	105
WYOMISSING AREA S D	76.70	932.63	31.02	204.61	162.91	54.91	60.00	1,583.78	68	1,704.87	105
COUNTY	55.95	840.95	31.93	192.15	150.09	57.28	40.56	1,368.91		1,575.34	
BLAIR											
ALTOONA AREA S D	34.49	773.04	32.06	150.88	124.89	40.07	68.59	1,224.01	368	1,363.50	412
BELLWOOD-ANTIS S D	55.75	607.15	17.29	164.65	109.63	57.77	57.77	1,048.61	500	1,194.19	496
CLAYSBURG-KIMMEL S D	53.79	719.65	17.19	173.43	134.13	96.38	44.06	1,131.02	424	1,193.02	421
HOLLIDAYSBURG AREA S D	39.28	744.58	81.21	154.25	104.86	63.03	35.28	1,172.59	424	1,319.59	444
SPRING COVE S D	39.29	697.09	21.13	135.81	126.15	86.36	33.62	1,140.66	457	1,496.24	264
TYRONE AREA S D	56.82	680.98	30.55	156.63	126.15	86.40	43.11	1,141.08	456	1,144.27	502
WILLIAMSBURG COMM S D	69.45	746.56	18.01	126.34	143.36	78.44	42.31	1,224.49	365	1,314.24	448
COUNTY	41.54	735.27	28.52	151.16	120.13	56.41	51.81	1,184.85		1,331.84	

Comparative Per Pupil Expenditures for Individual School Districts, 'Public School Financial Statistics Report, 1976-77, OUR SCHOOLS TODAY, VOL 17, No. 7, Pa. Department of Education, 1978, p. 38.

Illustration No. 21
STATE DESIGNATED BUDGET
CATEGORIES CHART OF ACCOUNTS

GENERAL FUND
CHART OF STANDARD EXPENDITURE ACCOUNTS

0100 ADMINISTRATION

0111 SALARIES, BOARD OFFICIALS
0112 SALARIES, EDUCATIONAL ADMINISTRATION
0113 SALARIES, BUSINESS ADMINISTRATION
0114 SALARIES, LEGAL SERVICES
0115 SALARIES, TAX COLLECTION
0121 MATERIALS AND SUPPLIES, ADMINISTRATION
0124 MATERIALS AND SUPPLIES, LEGAL SERVICES
0125 MATERIALS AND SUPPLIES, TAX COLLECTION
0131 EXPENSES, ADMINISTRATION
0134 EXPENSES, LEGAL SERVICES
0135 EXPENSES, TAX COLLECTION
0151 CONTRACTED AUDITING SERVICES
0154 CONTRACTED LEGAL SERVICES
0155 CONTRACTED TAX COLLECTION SERVICES
0159 OTHER CONTRACTED SERVICES FOR ADMINISTRATION

0200 INSTRUCTION

0211 SALARIES, PRINCIPALS
0212 SALARIES, SUPERVISORS OR COORDINATORS
0213 SALARIES, TEACHERS
0214 SALARIES, LIBRARIANS
0216 SALARIES, OTHER INSTRUCTIONAL STAFF
0218 SALARIES, INSTRUCTIONAL ASSISTANTS
0219 SALARIES, SECRETARIAL, CLERICAL, OTHER PERSONNEL
0221 TEXTBOOKS
0222 TEACHING SUPPLIES
0223 LIBRARY BOOKS AND SUPPLIES
0224 AUDIOVISUAL MATERIALS
0229 OTHER MATERIALS AND SUPPLIES FOR INSTRUCTION
0231 EXPENSES, IN-SERVICE TRAINING
0239 EXPENSES, OTHER, FOR INSTRUCTION
0250 CONTRACTED SERVICES FOR INSTRUCTION

0300 PUPIL PERSONNEL SERVICES

0311 SALARIES, DIRECTORS, COORDINATORS, SUPERVISORS
0312 SALARIES, ATTENDANCE PERSONNEL
0313 SALARIES, GUIDANCE & PSYCHOLOGICAL PERSONNEL
0319 SALARIES, CLERICAL AND OTHER CLASSIFIED PERSONNEL
0320 MATERIALS AND SUPPLIES, PUPIL PERSONNEL SERVICES
0330 EXPENSES, PUPIL PERSONNEL SERVICES
0350 CONTRACTED SERVICES, PUPIL PERSONNEL SERVICES

*Excerpt from summary pages of the Chart of Standard
Expenditures Accounts, Pennsylvania Department of Education.*

FINANCIAL POLICIES & PROCEDURES

CDE-HNB-F01   Section No: ACC/301   Page 1

Date Issued: **July 1, 1975**   Effective Date: **January 1, 1976**

Subject: **THE "EDUCATIONAL ACCOUNTABILITY ACT OF 1971"**
and the "FINANCIAL POLICIES AND PROCEDURES ACT"

I. **DIRECTIVES**

The "Educational Accountability Act of 1971":

"The general assembly hereby declares that the purpose of this article is to institute an accountability program to define and measure quality in education, and thus to help the public schools of Colorado to achieve such quality and to expand the life opportunities and options of the students of this state; further, to provide the local school boards assistance in helping their school patrons to determine the relative value of their school program as compared to its cost."

(Colorado Revised Statutes, 1973, 22-7-102(1))

The "Financial Policies and Procedures Act":

"It is the purpose of this article to develop for the public schools a program-oriented budget format which will relate anticipated costs and actual costs to designated programs."

(Colorado Revised Statutes, 1973, 22-44-202)

"The financial policies and procedures handbook so adopted shall be compatible with the provisions of the "Accountability Act of 1971", but shall be limited primarily to the relating of budgeted and actual costs to designated programs."

(Colorado Revised Statutes, 1973, 22-44-203(2))

II. **A LOCAL PROGRAM BUDGET: BASIC CONCEPTS**

Rationale: The function of program budgeting is to insure that school board members and school district personnel, in their deliberations and decisions about budgeting matters, develop a local program budget.

Basic Concepts: The following diagram presents the four basic concepts which relate program budgeting to the budgeting process.

Colorado Department of Education "Financial Policies and Procedures" p. 1

Illustration No. 22—(Continued)

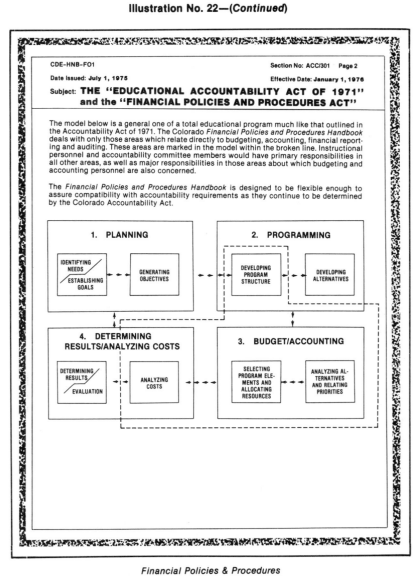

CDE-HNB-FO1   Section No: ACC/301   Page 2

Date Issued: **July 1, 1975**   Effective Date: **January 1, 1976**

Subject: **THE "EDUCATIONAL ACCOUNTABILITY ACT OF 1971"
and the "FINANCIAL POLICIES AND PROCEDURES ACT"**

The model below is a general one of a total educational program much like that outlined in the Accountability Act of 1971. The Colorado *Financial Policies and Procedures Handbook* deals with only those areas which relate directly to budgeting, accounting, financial reporting and auditing. These areas are marked in the model within the broken line. Instructional personnel and accountability committee members would have primary responsibilities in all other areas, as well as major responsibilities in those areas about which budgeting and accounting personnel are also concerned.

The *Financial Policies and Procedures Handbook* is designed to be flexible enough to assure compatibility with accountability requirements as they continue to be determined by the Colorado Accountability Act.

1. PLANNING

IDENTIFYING NEEDS / ESTABLISHING GOALS →← GENERATING OBJECTIVES

2. PROGRAMMING

DEVELOPING PROGRAM STRUCTURE →← DEVELOPING ALTERNATIVES

4. DETERMINING RESULTS/ANALYZING COSTS

DETERMINING RESULTS / EVALUATION →← ANALYZING COSTS

3. BUDGET/ACCOUNTING

SELECTING PROGRAM ELEMENTS AND ALLOCATING RESOURCES →← ANALYZING ALTERNATIVES AND RELATING PRIORITIES

Financial Policies & Procedures

— 65 —

to be used and describes briefly the items that may or may not be included in each expenditure category. It often appears as part of the State Financial and Accounting Manual, a huge volume that you may find helpful if you expect to review particular categories of expenses in any detail.

To study the budget process, you will want some additional documents. Write to the state department of education for the section of your state law relating to the school budget process. Other information should be available at the office of your local school board.

- The section of your state law relating to the school budget process (Illustration 22, pages 64 and 65).

- Your state's department of education regulations regarding the budget process (Illustration 5, page 19).

- All local board of education policies guiding the budget development process (Illustrations 7 and 8, pages 21, 22 and 23).

- The District Budget Calendar (Illustration 17, page 50).

- The chart—if one exists—that illustrates the budget process and indicates who is responsible for each step that is carried out (Illustrations 17, 18 and 19, pages 50, 51 and 52).

And finally, you'll want one more thing, the importance of which cannot be overemphasized. You need a notebook. Not scraps of paper to take notes on, but a permanent record—preferably in loose leaf form, so that you can add more pages if necessary—in which to keep all your notes from the very beginning of your budget studies. It is important to write down all your findings, all the questions that occur to you—everything that relates to your budget study. The notebook acts as a check on your memory and a prod to it, as well as providing a way of organizing the information you gather.

As soon as you have the notebook, start listing the documents you've asked for. Leave space for their official designations: what you call "Actual Expenditures" may be entitled officially "School Returns: Form DE597." And leave space to fill in the following information:

- When you made the request
- The person of whom you made it
- The information you received
- The person who sent it to you
- When the information was received.

If you do not receive the information you've asked for, note the following—if you have the necessary information—in your book:

- Why the person requested cannot give you the information
- Where, precisely, you can get it
- When, precisely, it will be available.

In-Person Visits

If it is at all possible, try to gather your information by going in person, rather than telephoning or writing. This serves two purposes. It gets you the information more quickly, and it shows you how well prepared any given education office is to respond to citizen requests for information on the budget. There is no need to make an appointment before going. If the office *is* well prepared, the secretary or receptionist will simply go to a file and hand you the information you've asked for.

When you introduce yourself, use your own name; don't introduce yourself in relationship to your child. You are there as a citizen, and your personal relationships and motivations require no explanation. There is nothing wrong with answering questions, if you want to. But if you don't want to, there is no reason why you should. Even though you have every right to this information, be cordial and friendly. In other words, be firm but pleasant. You never can tell when a friend in the lower part of the hierarchy will help you later on. There is no reason for you to see an administrator at this time. If the secretary insists that you talk to someone further up in the heirarchy, point out that you will be glad to, after you've had a chance to study the material you've asked for, but that it would be a waste of everyone's time at this point.

Visiting Your Neighborhood School

The best place to start gathering information is your own local school. Go to the secretary's office and ask for all the available information on the budget. You may be able to get only a very limited amount—the popularized budget or the current year's budget. But after you've gotten what's available, ask for every single item on your list by name, and note every answer you get about it.

Don't expect to get too much from your local school building. Most citizens report that they are unable to obtain anything. But check it out anyway. It says something about the accessibility of budget information to the average citizen. And it says something about the involvement—or lack of involvement—of the staff in budget matters, so don't be upset with the local school personnel if they don't have the information. You later may want to make some recommendations to your district on these points in the course of your budget study. Point out that not everyone can get to central school headquarters easily. Some people don't have cars, or have no time available during the day for long trips, or have small children to look after and can't be chasing all over. A really democratic process should make it possible for them to get budget information from a location that's reasonably accessible to them.

Visiting Central Headquarters

In seeking information from the central headquarters of your school district, the best place to start out is in the office of the superintendent. The secretary in that office ought to be able to go to the files and supply you with most of the information you want. If the superintendent's office does not have enough copies, you may have to go to the specific office that prepares the budget or oversees the district's financial matters. In larger school districts you may have to see an assistant superintendent for finance, a budget officer, a business manager, and/or a public information officer. Undoubtedly, all of these persons will have some information of interest to you, so make it a point to go to those offices and collect whatever they have.

Many school districts use newsletters or special mailings to inform their communities of the role citizens are invited to play in the budget process (Illustration 23, pages 72 and 73). They also may mail or make available minutes of school board meetings or budget meetings. When you are making your inquiries, ask for copies of such publications for the current year and the last two or three years. You may find, of course, that there are none, and that the school district has made no real effort to involve the community in the budget process. If this is the case, you may find yourself fighting an uphill battle for citizen participation. On the other hand, the failure of effort may be only an oversight; you may find your efforts received with open arms.

Another source for information on the community's role in the budget process is your local newspaper. The education editor or the reporter assigned to cover school affairs usually has a file with news releases from the school district and with stories that relate to the budget process. A good perspective can be gained from such material: it will help you learn, for example, whether citizen participation was sought early or late in the budget process; it may give you the names of persons who have testified on budget matters, and may also indicate which issues were resolved or left dangling by previous budget actions.

Make notes of what you get from central headquarters, where they tell you to go, and any other suggestions they may have for obtaining information. Again, do it on the spot and check it out. Write in your notebook and then say to the secretary or administrator, "Do I have this correct? You are going to have a copy of this made up and mailed out to me by tomorrow afternoon?" Or, "You only have your own file copy and you don't know where I can go to get a copy for my home study?" Or, "You will get this other information together, including the report on the needs assessment, last year's proposed and actual budgets, and the audit of actual expenditures, and I can come in again and pick it up at the end of the week?" Or, "You say no one has ever asked for this information before so there are no extra copies?" Or, "You say that no one is allowed to see the expenditures from last year because they are confidential?"

Writing to Gather Information

If you find it impossible to make in-person visits to gather printed information, both at your local school and the district headquarters, you will want to write a letter requesting information. You will want to write some follow-up letters also.

And if you are seeking information from your state's department of education or superintendent of public instruction, you will also need to write. Here are some hints you may find useful:

1. Use carbon paper (or a duplicating machine) so that you have three copies of each letter. The original goes to the person to whom you are writing. The second copy will be used as a follow-up. The third will be put in your permanent notebook.

2. Feel free to write by hand. After all, you are a citizen. . .and you don't have a secretary assigned to you to handle your correspondence! If you can write legibly, it is just as acceptable as typing, but, again, keep *two* copies for yourself.

3. If you are working with a group, identify yourself and the group. For example, "As the chairperson of the Budget Study Committee of the Centre City PTA, I wish to have the following information for use in our review of the budget. . .." Even if you're working on your own, you might say, "As an interested citizen and taxpayer, I wish. . .."

4. If you include your phone number and the times you can be reached, you may give immediate clarification if the official who received your letter needs it. On the other hand, it also might result in getting into conversation for which you aren't ready. You will have to weigh the pros and cons on this one.

5. Enclose a self-addressed, stamped envelope for a reply.

6. After making your specific request(s), always include a request for "Any additional information which will help clarify the budget or the budget process."

7. Indicate if you are willing to pick up the printed information once they advise you where and when, or if you are requesting that the information be mailed. You are bound to get a lot more informa-

tion if you can go to pick it up, but don't waste your time if they only have a five-page popularized budget, or budget calendar, to give you.

8. If your letter is a follow-up to a visit, refer to the visit and acknowledge the information already obtained. For example, "Thank you for giving me a copy of the 1976–77 Budget Summary when I stopped in your office on October 10th. Would you please send me the following additional material...."

9. Sample letters—There are any number of different approaches you may use in writing for information. The illustrated examples may suggest a few of these approaches (pages 76, 77 and 78).

Writing to obtain information is often less satisfactory than going in person, but occasionally you will be pleasantly surprised by prompt and complete responses to your written requests. Otherwise, be determined to follow up.

Follow-up

If you have written for information to your local school district and haven't heard *anything* within a week, follow up. If writing to state officials, allow at least two or three weeks.

The easiest follow-up consists of sending one of your copies of the letter to the same person you sent the first one, marked (with bright magic-marker) "Second Request October 19, 1978." Make a note on your own copy of the date you send the second request.

If your letter was addressed to the state department of education, try sending a note to your legislator in the state capitol, saying, "Enclosed is a copy of a request for information which I sent two weeks ago to the state department of education. Would you kindly forward the copy to the department, asking them to send me a reply? Thank you for your assistance."

If you don't know the name and address of your state legislator call your local library's reference desk or the Election Office in your local courthouse. Your U.S. Congressman probably won't be of much help.

Illustration No. 23
BUDGET DEVELOPMENT

1975–76 BUDGET DEVELOPMENT PROCESS

A school budget, much like a family budget, is a set of guidelines developed to operate the schools within the expected income for a one-year period. Many steps and many people are involved before a school budget is approved by the School Board.

The Administration has begun preparation of the 1975–76 budget under a Board guideline to consider as first alternative that estimated receipts equal estimated expenditures (balanced budget with no reserve fund). In a series of meetings, the Instructional Council Budget Review Committee and other groups are providing the Administration with reaction and input to the budget development as it progresses.

Budget information as of November 15, 1974, enrollment projections for 75–76 and the current state financing laws, constitute the departure point and a 12% inflation rate is being used to develop budget projections.

Certain given factors are the basis for the budget development, such as State laws, State Department of Education regulations, School Board policy, negotiated contract provisions, and administrative regulations.

For instance, in arriving at the number of instructional staff for each school, the above given factors must be considered. In determining the per pupil allocation of money to each school, which is earmarked for instructional and other recurring supplies and does not include teacher or other staff salaries, again State laws and regulations, etc. have to be considered.

The budget preparation is proceeding under a School Board approved time schedule; completion is slated for late January of 1975. Between December 3 and 11 a series of informational meetings have been planned (see schedule in this issue) to familiarize residents of the district with 75–76 budget projections and alternative solutions which are being considered to deal with the financial situation.

Another series of meetings will be held in January of 1975 to answer questions raised during the December meetings and to discuss alternative solutions.

ALTERNATIVE SOLUTIONS

DEFICIT SPENDING

Deficit spending is considered by many a possible or acceptable avenue to finance school operations and thus alleviate the pressures of curtailing or eliminating programs and services now being provided. That course of action would require the sale of certificates of indebtedness. Interest would need to be paid on these certificates out of the general fund receipts. Sale of certificates of indebtedness, in effect, means to borrow from the following year's income.

An advance for general fund expenditures can be obtained from the following year's anticipated general fund receipts. This, too, is a form of loan, determined in amount by the Ramsey County Auditor and which requires no interest. For instance, if the district made use of the possibility of an advance for the 1975–76 school year, the amount would be available in June of 1976. The amount advanced would be deducted from the July, 1976 tax distribution.

INCREASING THE TAX LEVY

State law allows local districts the option of holding a referendum to increase the local tax levy over and above the limit established by the State Legislature. To increase the tax levy, the district would need to ask the taxpayers for a 'yes' vote on a tax levy referendum to increase the property taxes for district residents. Assuming that such a referendum would pass, the additional income would not be available to the district until the fiscal year following its approval by district residents. The district would receive 100 per cent of the taxes approved by a levy referendum. There would be no reduction in State foundation aids if the voters authorized an additional levy.

LEGISLATIVE ACTIONS

The Legislature can choose to increase aid per pupil for school districts by legislative action. If the Legislature should authorize an increase in foundation aid before June 30, 1975, the increase of aid per pupil times the number of students in District 621 could be available for the 1975–76 school year. The School Board, administration and members of the Instructional Council have been involved in an effort to inform legislative representatives of the District's financial situation and the pressing need for State legislative action to ensure continued excellence in education.

Mounds View (Minn) "School Talk" Special Issue.

If you have been told to expect the material you requested within a week, follow up within two or three days of the appointed time with a phone call. Again, note carefully to whom you speak, and ask him to get back to you within a day or two with the information requested. Say, "You (or he) promised to have that information to me by yesterday. Can I count on hearing from *you* by noon tomorrow?"

Illustration No. 23—(*Continued*)

CURTAILING OR ELIMINATING PROGRAMS AND SERVICES

Without clear indication at this point that the Legislature will make a strong shift toward major changes in the school financing laws, with spiraling costs and with a projected deficit of 2.6 million dollars at the end of 1976, consideration must be given to curtailing or eliminating programs and services in every function of the district's operation in order to balance expenditures with income. Responsible financial management becomes extremely difficult when choices which need to be made not only affect people and their livelihood, but have a direct bearing on the purpose of existence of everyone in the district's employ: education and the programs and opportunities the district provides for its students.

AWARENESS AND INVOLVEMENT

The budget development at this point involves only cost projections for 1975-76 on the basis of programs and services presently being provided. Every effort is being made to involve as many groups as possible within the district to become aware, to reason together, and to arrive at decisions which will best preserve the educational goals of the School Board, staff, administration, students, and parents of the district.

The School Board, staff and administration of the district urge citizens, parents, students, legislative representatives and city officials to attend one of the meetings scheduled for December. The dates, times and places for the series of meetings planned for January will be announced at a later date.

PUBLIC MEETINGS SCHEDULED

Following are dates, times, and places of meetings to which citizens are invited:

Tuesday, December 3
Highview Junior High School, 2300 7th Street N.W., New Brighton
4:15 p.m. and 7:30 p.m.

Wednesday, December 4
Chippewa Junior High School, 5000 Hodgson Road, St. Paul
4:00 p.m.
Mounds View Senior High School, 1900 W. County Road F, St. Paul
7:30 p.m.

Thursday, December 5
District Service Center, 2959 N. Hamline Ave., Roseville
9:30 a.m.
Edgewood Junior High School, 5100 N. Edgewood Drive, New Brighton
4:00 p.m. and 7:30 p.m.

Saturday, December 7
Chippewa Junior High School, 5000 Hodgson Road, St. Paul
8:00 a.m.

Monday, December 9
Irondale Senior High School, 2425 Long Lake Road, New Brighton
4:00 p.m.

Tuesday, December 10
Chippewa Junior High School, 5000 Hodgson Road, St. Paul
1:30 p.m. and 7:30 p.m.

Wednesday, December 11
District Service Center, 2959 N. Hamline Ave., Roseville
8:00 a.m. and 1:00 p.m.
Johanna Junior High School, 1910 W. County Road D, St. Paul
7:30 p.m.

Mounds View (Minn) "School Talk" Special Issue.

Right-to-Know and Freedom of Information Laws

After you have exhausted these strategies and still are denied the specific documents you requested, don't despair. Most states have "Right-to-Know" laws which may be of help. You can bring to your local officials' attention the state law that applies. It helps if you cite the particular section of the law under which you are requesting the information. Although it is not always possible or necessary, a letter from an attorney may bring prompt disclosure, particularly in instances in which bureaucratic red-tape has prevented your access to the documents you've requested.

In most states, the "Right-to-Know" law allows any citizen to inspect a public record. The citizen need not demonstrate any personal interest in the record nor give a reason for requesting it. Requests for information must be specific and should name the document requested. Thus, the salary of each individual employee of a school district is open to inspection, as is the collective bargaining agreement between the school district and any group of employees. So are accounts recording the expenditures of funds and the minutes of the meeting in which the superintendent presented his budget proposal to the board. The transfers of funds from one budgetary account to another are available to you in the minutes of the board and, if your school district's internal procedure requires it, in "Transfer Authorizations."

The federal "Freedom of Information Act" (FOIA) applies only to agencies of the federal government. But if a local school district received money for educational programs from the U.S. Office of Education and/or other federal agencies, information about these programs is available under the FOIA, either by publication or by inspection of records. If you are interested in records concerning a program which receives federal funds you should be able to obtain from the federal agency involved all the information transmitted by your local school district including correspondence between the agency and the district.

If you wish to obtain or inspect a public record in the possession of a federal agency, the first step is to request the specific record from the agency. Each agency is supposed to establish regulations setting forth specific procedures (e.g. whom to contact) to be followed in requesting information; these regulations are published in the *Federal Register*, but in some cases an agency might tell you the procedure by telephone. The agency is required to respond to your request within ten days. In some circumstances an agency may extend these time limits an additional ten days if it notifies you in writing of the reasons for the extension and the date on which you may expect a response.

Dealing With Delay

Citizens seeking budget information from foot-dragging school districts report considerable success in obtaining information after citing "Right-to-Know" and "Freedom of Information" laws to their local officials. If there is unreasonable delay in obtaining material and you are given no logical explanation there are a number of strategies you might consider using:

1. If a clerical person seems to be uninformed request an explanation from her/his boss.

2. If a lower level administrator delays, make an appointment to see the superintendent.

3. If the superintendent causes the delays, call one or more members of the school board to find out what their policy is and if they (as your elected representative) condone the delays.

4. Consider bringing long delays to the attention of the board at its next public board meeting. (Find out in advance if you have to register to speak, if you must have a written statement, and what time you can speak.) If you do this, your presentation may be designed to request the board to adopt a policy that makes budget and financial information fully and promptly available to citizens. Remember that this may result in embarrassing the school administration (which may or may not suit your long-range purpose).

Make Your Own Copies: Use commercial photocopy services or, if you really can't get a copy of the material you want, consider renting or borrowing a portable, desk-top photocopy machine. This is about the size of a typewriter and can be operated easily. It will copy about 10 pages in 15–20 minutes, after which it must be allowed to cool down for awhile. At $20 for 200 sheets of paper, each copy will cost you 10¢. This is a last resort strategy because it still takes time, though not as much as copying every item by hand. The copies may not be as good as those which the school itself can make or as good as those a commercial copying service will make for you if the school lends you a file copy. "Right-to-Know" laws usually allow such copying.

THE SCHOOL BUDGET

Example 1.
Sample letter to obtain information locally.

January 10, 1979

Superintendent of Schools
Center City School District
Center City, State, Zip

Dear Sir/Madam:

As a citizen interested in the Center City School District budget, I would appreciate receiving the following information:

1. The 1978-79 Budget (including the estimated expenditures for 1978-79 and the actual expenditures and income for 1977-78).

2. The 1977-78 Budget

3. The 1976-77 Budget

4. Any additional information you have that explains the budget, analyzes the figures in the budget, or contains information related to the budget which may not be included in the budget document.

I have enclosed a self-addressed, stamped envelope to facilitate your prompt reply, telling me when I may expect to receive the material. If the material is too voluminous to mail, I will be happy to pick up the material if your reply indicates when and where this can be done.

Sincerely yours,

Mary Smith
1234 Main Street
Center City, State, Zip

Phone: 555-3456
         After 7:00 p.m.

NOTE: Write separate letters for material which is likely to come out of different departments or bureaus.

Example 2.
Sample letter to obtain information from the state

January 10, 1979

Commissioner of Education
State Department of Education
Capital City, State, Zip

Dear Sir:

The Citizens Committee for Better Education in Center
City is seeking information to help us in our study of school
budgets and educational expenditures. Please send us the following material:

1. State-wide financial statistics, including per-pupil
expenditures in various categories on a district-by-district
breakdown.

2. Any additional statistical information which your
office has which would be helpful in our study.

We will, of course, be in touch with our local district
officials to obtain information on local details.

Thank you for your prompt attention to this request. If
there will be any delay in fulfilling this request, please contact
me at the address or telephone listed below.

Very truly yours,

Mary Smith
Citizen for Better Education
1234 Main Street
Center City, State, Zip

Phone: 800-555-3456
        (9-3 p.m.)

NOTE: *Write separate letters for material which is likely to come out of different departments or bureaus.*

Example 3.
Sample letter to obtain information from the state

January 11, 1979

Superintendent of Public Instruction
State Department of Public Instruction
Captial City, State, Zip

Dear Sir:

The Citizens Committee for Better Education in Center
City is seeking information to help us in our study of school
budgets and educational expenditures. Please send us the following material:

1. An explanation of the state aid to local school
   districts.

2. Any additional information which your office has
   which would be helpful in our study.

Thank you for your prompt attention to this request.
If there will be any delay in fulfilling this request, please
contact me at the address or telephone listed below:

Very truly yours,

Mary Smith, Citizens
for Better Education
1324 Main Street
Center City, State, Zip
Area Code 800-555-3456
(9 - 3 p.m.)

NOTE: *Write separate letters for material which is likely to come out of different departments or bureaus.*

Schools should meet your requests promptly and fully. In some school districts copies will be made for you at no charge. In a few you may have to pay the photocopy charge. If this happens, ask how many copies originally were made and to whom these have been distributed. If 25 or 100 were made to distribute to board members and major administrators, some still may be around for you to borrow. Also, you then can go to the board and suggest that they authorize the printing of another dozen copies or another 100 copies (depending on the size of the school district). Also ask about receiving regularly copies of the prior months' budget reports as the board receives updates. You might point out that such authorization would demonstrate the board's responsiveness to citizen interest.

Inadequate Information: Finally, you may learn that some of the information basic for your understanding of the school budget and the budget process is simply not in existence. That is, not only unavailable to you, but also unavailable to the board or the superintendent as part of the decision-making process. If that is the case, the entire school budget process is clearly in need of improvement. If you are to work effectively towards that end, it is important that you have the facts clear and that your notes are complete i.e., "Let me get this straight. You said you can't give me a copy of the board's budget priorities because there isn't any?" Or "Did I understand you correctly? Did you say, 'There is no written record of the needs assessment for the school district because we do that on an informal basis.'?"

Once you have obtained any printed information, plan to start reviewing it promptly. Again, make careful notes. Write down questions you have about the material. Write down reminders to seek additional back-up information. If you are working on a budget analysis, start preparing the worksheets (they are described in chapter 7 of this book.) If you are working on the budget process, start preparing a chart or a step-by-step description of your district's process. And, meanwhile, plan to follow up on the requests for printed information that have not yet been met.

Learning About the Internal Budget Process In Your School District

Call the central administrative headquarters of your school district and ask who is the budget officer. In small districts it may be the superintendent; in larger ones it may be the business manager, or an assistant, associate or deputy superintendent for finance. Then call this person and tell him or her that you would like to make an appointment to learn about the school budget process. Ask to have any printed material relating to the budget process sent to you before your appointment. (Some of what you get may duplicate material you already have, in which case you can return it when you go for your appointment.) Assure the budget officer that you do not mind reading difficult material or administrative jargon; assure him or her that you would welcome such material as well as any popularized descriptions of the budget process that may be available.

Before your appointment, review the material you have collected, go over the budget process list and the list of "Budget Review Questions" in this book, and arrange to have someone else go along with you. If possible, take along a tape recorder. Be certain you have it ready to use and that you can use it easily. Many libraries will lend you one.

At the beginning of your interview, let the budget officer know that you will be taping the interview to be certain you get everything right. Reassure him or her that you will not be using the tapes for broadcasting and that you would be happy to reserve a little time at the end of the interview for any "off-the-record" comments he/she might want to make.

Be prepared to listen carefully, take notes and ask questions. You may want to have a number of questions prepared before you go into the interview. Find out with whom the Budget Officer works most closely during the budget formulation process. Be specific. Ask *who* figures out the anticipated state aid. Ask *who* prepared the estimates of expenditures for the elementary schools. Ask *who* prepares the estimates for insurance costs. Ask *who* suggests the figures to be put in the budget for salaries if no collective bargaining agreement is in effect for the forthcoming year. To whom does he/she report? Who reports to the Budget Officer?

Leave the door open to return or call after you have digested the information you have gathered. Find out if the Budget Officer would have any objections if you called the people specifically responsible for particular budget responsibilities. Remember that, at this stage, you are *learning* about the internal budget process; you are not trying to participate in it nor (at this point) trying to improve upon it.

You will find it very helpful to chart the budget process based on what you have learned from the printed material and interviews. There may be discrepancies and contradictions, but once you have it all drawn out on

Illustration No. 24
CHART OF BUDGET PROCESS

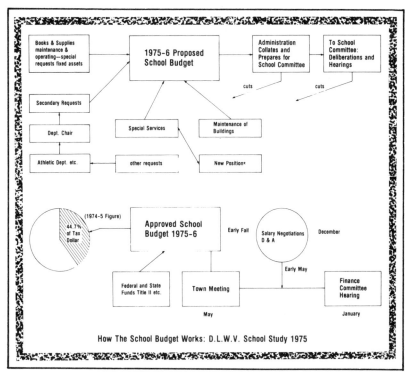

How The School Budget Works: D.L.W.V. School Study 1975

*Adapted from a chart of the budget process of Dedham Schools,
prepared by the League of Women Voters of Dedham, Mass., 1975*

paper, you will know which points need further inquiry. The Dedham
League of Women Voters (Illustration 24, above) [1] and the D.C.
Citizens for Better Education prepared such budget process charts.

If your school district has a budget process chart, find out when it was
adopted. Find out also which activities and steps are quietly skipped and
what has been added (Illustrations 17 and 18, pages 50 and 51).

Don't be discouraged if you are not immediately successful in
understanding the internal budget process. It may be that the process in

your district is haphazard and poorly organized. It may be that the explanations given to you are deliberately unclear. It may be that, because of the size of the school district or the sophisticated managerial processes it uses, a comprehensive understanding of the budget process will take a lot more homework from you. In the latter case, take heart! Probably no one else (including some of the board members and many high officials within the district) has a good grasp of the process either. But with persistence, determination and effort you may be able to develop a unique and useful knowledge of the internal budget process.

Footnotes
(Chapter 6)

[1] Dedham League of Women Voters, LOCAL SCHOOL STUDY COMMITTEE ANNUAL REPORT 1974-75. Dedham, Mass. 1975.

Chapter 7

The Budget Worksheets:
Finding the Facts in the Figures

AND NOW WE COME TO the part of the budget process in which you take out your pocket calculator and use it to transform all those rows and columns of figures in the school budget into useful information about the state of education in your school district. In this chapter, we're actually going to analyze some budget figures and do some comparative studies to see what we can learn from them.

Let's begin with the revenue figures. As mentioned earlier, they are generally the best place to start. But first, let's talk briefly about one item in those figures that generally forms a significant share of the school revenue and that often provides parents and citizens with their first incentive to become interested in the school budget. That item is, as we are sure you know, property taxes.* It's not our function to tell you how high or low they should be. We want merely to set out some facts for you, and to offer a few cautions.

As we have found with practically everything about the school budget, there is no single set of uniform regulations that governs either the way property taxes are set or their rate. It is up to you to find out *how* they are set in your community—whether the school board has the power to set them; whether they are set by your city (or town) council; and whether the tax rates or the budget must be approved by the voters.

However they are set, the base on which they are calculated is the *assessed* value of each piece of property, a value which is determined in most communities by a county official. The assessed value of a piece of property is not necessarily the same thing as its market (or true) value—the amount for which it would sell on the open market. In most communities, as a matter of fact, it is generally considerably less: 35% of

---

*State aid in some school districts constitutes an even more significant share.

market value is a pretty standard figure. At 35%, a house that cost $30,000, for example, would have an assessed value of $10,500.

The unit of currency on which property taxes are figured is the mill—one tenth of one cent or one thousandth of a dollar ($.001). If the school tax on property in your community is 50 mills for every dollar of assessed value, and property is assessed at 35% of market value, you will pay a yearly school tax of $525 on your $30,000 house (.001 × 50 × $10,500).

But there is nothing sacred about that 35% figure, either. The assessed value may be set at 50% of market value, so that a $30,000 house has an assessed value of $15,000. It may even be 100%—in which case, the assessed value and the market value are supposedly the same. We raise this point for a specific reason. Officials who set property tax rates—whether they are school board members or city council members—will sometimes boast that they have lowered the property tax rate, thereby trying to give the impression that the tax itself has been lowered, too. But that isn't necessarily the case. If property in your community is assessed at 100% of market value and your house cost $30,000, a drop in the property tax rate from 50 mills to 25 mills will still leave you paying $750 a year in school taxes while your friend in a neighboring community whose house cost the same and whose tax is 50 mills, but whose property is assessed at 35% of market value will be paying $525.

One final point: Since taxes are levied on the assessed valuation of property, the effects of inflation raise a serious issue. Suppose, for example, that your neighbors bought their house ten years before you bought yours, during a time of generally lower prices, and paid $15,000 for it. If the community assessed at 35% of its market value, its assessed valuation is $5,250. And this means, of course, that it carries a considerably lower property tax than yours. The obvious way of dealing with such inequities is to have local property reassessed periodically. And, in fact, more and more communities are doing just that. Since the assessor usually operates on the principle that the selling price of a property is its market value, the price of the house most recently sold in the community is likely to determine the value of a house similar to it—assuming, of course, that they are in the same state of repair.

The Revenue Worksheets

On the following pages you will find samples of the revenue sections of the school budget for a particular district for the fiscal years 1978, 79 and 80, and also a sample of the proposed budget for 1980. Using them as a basis for computation, we're going to make up some worksheets that will answer—and also raise—the kinds of questions you're likely to be interested in.

How much additional or reduced revenue is anticipated from the various sources of revenue as compared to prior years? Are these figures realistic? If no explanation accompanies the revenue estimates, you will have to raise questions including:

a. Is the change in local property tax revenue due to change in the tax rate? In the assessment rate? In the market value of real estate in the district? If you are in a growing community, does the budget figure take into account the anticipated increase in market value (and therefore assessed valuation on which taxes will be levied)?

b. Are there additional taxes which the local district could levy other than real estate/property taxes? For example, wage taxes, income taxes, occupation taxes, mercantile taxes, sales tax, per capita taxes. If taxes are levied on income or on wages, does the anticipated revenue figure increase proportionately as wages are expected to increase?

c. Are the state grants listed in the budget increased as the legislature makes changes to provide additional funds? Are federal funds accurately anticipated?

d. Is the cash balance based on an up-to-date accounting?

Revenue Worksheet R-I:
Analyzing the Proposed Budget Revenue

Look at the excerpt from Budget-D, Proposed Budget for 1980–81 (page 87). Note that column 3 indicates the receipts anticipated for the forthcoming school year. It is these revenues that are to provide funds for the expenditures of the school district during 1980–81. In column 2 the amount of

Worksheet R-1

RECEIPTS

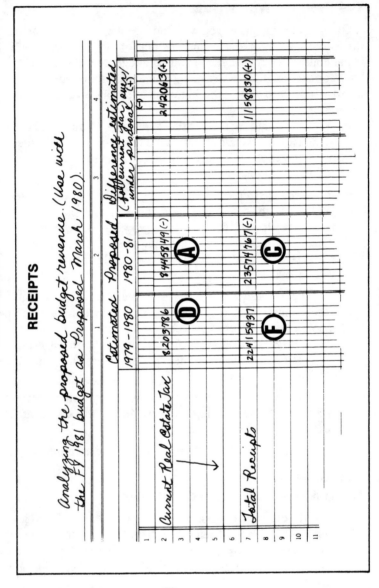

Analyzing the proposed budget revenue. (Use with the FY 1981 budget as Proposed March 1980).

	Estimated 1979-1980	Proposed 1980-81	Difference estimated (following year) under proposal (+)(-)
	1	2	3 & 4
1			
2 Current Real Estate Tax	8203786	8445849 (-)	242063 (+)
3			
4			
5		D	A
6			
7 Total Receipts	22415937	23574767 (-)	1158830 (+)
8		F	C
9			
10			
11			

BUDGET D
(Proposed Budget for 1980–81)

RECEIPTS

	1 ("Actual" Column 1 Missing)	2 Estimated 1979–1980	3 Proposed 1980–81 (As prepared March 1980)
FROM LOCAL SOURCES			Ⓐ
Current Real Estate Taxes		$ 8,203,786.00	$ 8,445,849.00
Public Utility Realty Tax		62,422.00	62,000.00
Current Per Capita Tax		195,000.00	193,200.00
Current Special Head Tax		390,000.00	386,400.00
Earned Income Tax		1,368,000.00	1,370,000.00
Real Estate Transfer Tax		—	27,500.00
Occupational Privilege Tax		—	245,000.00
In Lieu of Taxes		30,350.00	30,000.00
Delinquent Taxes and Penalties		392,500.00	426,000.00
Tuition, Non-Residents		27,000.00	27,000.00
Interest		151,500.00	150,000.00
Rentals		176,673.00	216,800.00
Sale of Real Estate & Equipment		1,000.00	61,000.00
Miscellaneous Revenue		16,500.00	15,000.00
Total Local Sources		$11,014,731.00	$11,655,749.00
Beginning Cash Balance		$ 170,477.00 Ⓔ	$ 334,672.00 Ⓑ
TOTAL RECEIPTS		$22,415,937.00 Ⓕ	$23,574,767.00 Ⓒ

revenue for the current year is listed. This column is called "Estimated 1979-1980." It is "estimated" because the proposed budget was made up in March 1980 and the current school year runs from July 1979 through June 1980. Some of the revenue, therefore, will not have been received by the time the proposed budget is prepared. The best the budget makers can do is enter the estimated revenue. And this they have done in Column 2.* Virtually no school districts budget on a calendar year basis (January-December); thus, if your state has a financial year that runs from July 1 to June 30, a 1980-81 budget (or Fiscal Year '81) begins July 1, 1980 and ends June 30, 1981.

Step 1: Notice that column 3 of Budget D anticipates approximately $8.4 million in real estate taxes (A), a beginning balance of $334,672 (B) and total receipts of $23,574,767 (C). We have entered the figures (A) and (C) on worksheet R-1 (page 86).

Step 2: Compare these figures with their equivalents in column 2 of Budget D. Here the real estate taxes are estimated at $8,203,786 (D), the beginning cash balance at $170,477 (E), and total receipts at $22,415,937 (F). We have entered some of these figures on worksheet R-1. Apparently, the budget makers anticipate increases of, respectively, $242,063; and $1,158,830, which we figured on our hand-held calculator and entered on the worksheet.

Step 3: You may want to compare the other items, to see just where the school officials anticipate additional—or less—revenue. If you enter these items on the worksheet you will then be ready to proceed.

Step 4: Now you are ready to look into the question of where the increased (or decreased) amounts of money are coming from. The proposed budget itself may carry explanations of the increases or decreases. If not, you may want to question your school officials directly. Does the anticipated increase in property tax revenue, for example, represent income from additional assess-

---

*Notice also that there is no column 1—the column in which the actual receipts for year ending July 1978 would normally be entered for comparative purposes.

ments—from the sale of new property or from an increase in the percent of market value on which assessments are made—or from an increase in the tax rate?

Cash Balance or Surplus: Most budgets include an anticipated beginning cash balance which may be a surplus or a deficit. Because the budget is prepared long before the year ends, this amount in very tentative. As the time for budget adoption draws closer, this amount is, or should be, revised to reflect a more accurate estimate. As in Worksheet R-2 (page 90), you can examine previous budgets to see how close to the budgeted amounts the actual balances were. However, if you want to testify or comment on a proposed budget and its projected revenues in March, it would be far more revealing for you to go back to the school board minutes or obtain elsewhere the previous years' *proposed* budgets (as they were first made public), to compare the cash balance figures included in the *adopted* budget, and then to compare both of these to the *actual* cash balance figures for the years covered by the budget. Note that the proposed budgets are not always readily available once the revised budget is actually adopted.

Revenue Worksheet R-2
Comparing Budgeted Revenue with Actual Revenue

In previous years, how close have the budgeted revenue amounts come to the actual amounts received? Has there been a pattern of underestimating revenue?

For this computation, you will need copies of the budget for at least two or three prior years. They should contain at least three columns: the budgeted figures for the forthcoming year, the estimated figures for the current year, and the actual figures for the previous year. If the "actuals" are missing, you will have to obtain the figures from the school district's annual audit or annual school report for the appropriate year. For the purposes of this exercise, we're going to use only Budgets A (page 96), B (page 91), and C (page 92).

Step 1: On your worksheet, list a column for Budgeted Revenue 1976-1977, a column for 1976-77 Actual Revenue, and a column for the difference (over or under). Do the same for the

Worksheet R—2

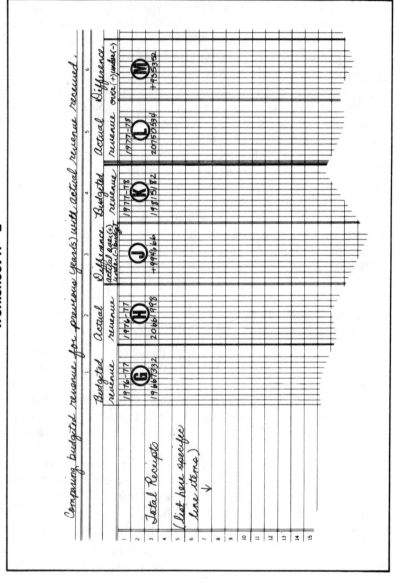

Comparing budgeted revenue for previous year(s) with actual revenue received.

	1 Budgeted revenue	2 Actual revenue	3 Difference actual over(+) (under-) budget	4 Budgeted revenue	5 Actual revenue	6 Difference actual over(+)(under-)
	G 1976-'77	**H** 1976-'77	**J** 1976-'77	**K** 1977-'78	**L** 1977-'78	**M**
1						
2 Total Receipts	1966'7332	2066'7998	+994'666	1981'51'82	2075'0'534	+95'3'52
3						
4 (list here specific line items)						
5 ↓						
6						
7						
8						
9						
10						
11						
12						
13						
14						
15						

BUDGET B
(FY 1979)

RECEIPTS
(September—June 30, 1978)

FROM LOCAL SOURCES	ACTUAL 1976-1977	ESTIMATED 1977-1978	BUDGETED 1978-1979
Current Real Estate Taxes.............	$ 5,278,148.31	$ 5,249,169.00	$ 6,725,059.00
Public Utility Realty Tax................	80,724.00	70,166.00	70,000.00
Current Per Capita Tax	188,934.67	190,000.00	190,000.00
Current Special Head Tax	377,869.04	380,000.00	380,000.00
Earned Income Tax....................	1,176,864.39	1,330,000.00	1,300,000.00
In Lieu of Taxes	28,434.42	26,380.00	25,000.00
Delinquent Taxes & Penalties..........	389,828.86	520,600.00	405,500.00
Tuition, Non-Residents	38,524.44	53,000.00	50,000.00
Interest on Investments................	123,216.54	200,000.00	100,000.00
Rentals................................	88,980.50	100,000.00	106,000.00
Sale of Surplus Equipment.............	1,834.87	200.00	1,000.00
Miscellaneous Revenue	10,302.61	10,000.00	10,000.00
Total Local Sources	$ 7,783,662.65	$ 8,129,515.00	$ 9,362,559.00
FROM STATE SOURCES			
Basic Instructional Subsidy............	$ 8,439,035.08	$ 8,664,316.00	$ 9,308,384.00
Homebound Instruction................	3,700.19	3,500.00	3,500.00
Special Education	468,025.85	235,000.00	225,000.00
Transportation........................	24,903.62	30,000.00	30,000.00
Vocational Education	87,916.58	140,000.00	146,000.00
Rentals and Sinking Fund Payments...	688,126.02	500,000.00	535,000.00
Driver Education......................	14,770.00	17,735.00	17,000.00
Medical and Dental Services	21,202.80	20,000.00	20,000.00
Nurse Services	61,841.50	60,000.00	60,000.00
Driver Improvement (Adult)	3,685.20	3,627.00	3,600.00
Extra Grant to School System	—	—	100,000.00
Total State Sources..................	$ 9,813,206.84	$ 9,674,178.00	$10,448,484.00
FROM FEDERAL SOURCES			
Equipment, NDEA	$ 10,644.08	$ 22,708.00	$ 27,000.00
Flood Loss............................	281,773.26	—	—
Adult Basic Education	42,428.32	61,000.00	72,150.00
E.S.E.	754,021.65	570,000.00	511,000.00
Other Federal Grants..................	23,991.01	11,133.00	35,000.00
Total Federal Sources	$ 1,112,858.32	$ 664,841.00	$ 645,150.00
REFUNDS—Prior Year's Expenditures...	$ 7,849.74	$ 51,680.00	$ 15,200.00
TUITION—From Other Districts	$ 23,535.76	$ 21,300.00	$ 20,000.00
Payroll Payable.......................	289,334.53	—	—
Revenue Received in Advance.........	28,638.94	—	—
Total Income From Other Sources...	$ 397,201.60	$ 177,053.00	$ 136,925.29
Beginning Cash Balance...............	$ 1,523,683.49	$ 1,607,209.70	$ 543,969.67
TOTAL RECEIPTS .... Ⓟ Ⓗ	$20,661,998.40	$19,975,776.70	$21,137,087.96

Ⓡ

BUDGET C
(FY 1978)

RECEIPTS

FROM LOCAL SOURCES	ACTUAL 1975-1976	ESTIMATED 1976-1977	BUDGETED 1977-1978
Current Real Estate Taxes	$ 6,426,135.06	$ 5,288,000.00	$ 5,224,169.00
Public Utility Realty Tax	64,054.00	80,724.00	80,000.00
Current Per Capita Tax	188,343.91	186,200.00	185,000.00
Current Special Head Tax	376,687.70	372,400.00	370,000.00
Earned Income Tax	1,114,050.09	1,200,000.00	1,330,000.00
In Lieu of Taxes	24,398.23	28,434.00	30,000.00
Delinquent Taxes & Penalties	353,038.81	357,000.00	567,600.00
Tuition, Non-Residents	38,639.33	35,000.00	35,000.00
Interest on Investments	80,665.95	100,000.00	125,000.00
Rentals	47,389.00	88,700.00	143,000.00
Gifts & Requests	2,978.33	—	
Sale of Surplus Equipment	81.21	1,200.00	1,000.00
Miscellaneous Revenue	224,057.18	10,000.00	10,000.00
Total Local Sources	$ 8,940,518.80	$ 7,747,658.00	$ 8,100,769.00
FROM STATE SOURCES			
Basic Instructional Subsidy	$ 7,590,227.22	$ 8,439,035.00	$ 8,664,316.00
Homebound Instruction	6,392.04	3,700.00	3,500.00
Special Education	201,277.88	444,800.00	200,000.00
Transportation	20,930.86	24,903.00	25,000.00
Vocational Education	133,968.99	160,000.00	140,000.00
Rentals and Sinking Fund Payments	425,389.53	634,003.00	550,000.00
Driver Education	14,665.00	14,770.00	14,000.00
Medical and Dental Services	21,382.80	21,203.00	20,000.00
Nurse Services	62,366.50	61,842.00	60,000.00
Driver Improvement (Adult)	2,774.40	2,700.00	—
Extra Grant to School System	44,450.11	—	—
Total State Sources	$ 8,523,825.33	$ 9,806,956.00	$ 9,676,816.00
FROM FEDERAL SOURCES			
Equipment, NDEA	$ 7,617.76	$ 10,644.00	$ —
Adult Basic Education	37,949.91	36,000.00	3,500.00
ESEA Title I	686,118.92	600,000.00	570,000.00
Other Federal Grants	37,989.09	6,000.00	—
Total Federal Sources	$ 769,675.68	$ 652,644.00	$ 573,500.00
REFUNDS—Prior Year's Expenditures	$ 7,442.85	$ 7,700.00	$ 5,000.00
TUITION—From Other Districts	$ 21,236.20	$ 20,000.00	$ 20,000.00
Total Income From Other Sources	$ 226,904.51	$ 81,294.00	—
Beginning Cash Balance	$ 1,769,338.89	$ 1,523,683.49	$ 1,439,097.10 Ⓚ
TOTAL RECEIPTS	$20,258,942.26	$19,839,935.49	$19,815,182.10

Ⓝ

other years for which you have budget and actual figures. Start with the total receipts and list the amounts. Note that item G on the worksheet is not illustrated in the budget. It was obtained from the school district. Item H can be found in the 1st column of Budget B. Item J is worksheet column 2 minus column 1. The total receipts for the Fiscal Year 1978 (1977–1978) Actual are taken from Budget A and shown as Item L in column 5. The Budgeted amount is taken from Budget C and shown in column 4 as item K. The difference between the two is shown in column 6 as item M.

Step 2: If the difference between total revenue budgeted and the actual revenue received is significant, check out each additional line of the revenue budget to see if the Real Estate Tax, the state basic subsidy or federal funds are regularly misestimated.

Step 3: Find out why these over or underestimations exist. If the state or federal government made new appropriations through legislative actions after the budget was adopted, this would account for some difference. If the Real Estate Property Tax receipts are always estimated on the basis of an 85% collection rate when, in fact, there is usually a 93% to 95% collection rate, this would account for a difference on this line item. Similarly, if Real Estate Taxes are always budgeted as resulting from a 5% increased assessment when your community is experiencing a 10% residential or commercial building growth each year, this could account for a pattern of underestimation.

Step 4: Now, look again at the proposed budget for the forthcoming year. Could it be that school officials are once again underestimating certain line items or the total amounts? If so, what difference would this make in the amount of money available for new programs, improvements or reduced taxes? On the illustrated Worksheet R–2 the total receipts were underestimated each year by more than $900,000, or about 4% or 5%. If this amount was added to the proposed 1980–1981 budget illustrated, it would mean an additional $950,000 for new programs, or a local property tax reduction of about 3 mills (in the community illustrated each mill of taxes produces about $312,000.)

Revenue Worksheet R-3:
Gauging the Accuracy of Estimated Revenue

In previous years, how close have the *estimated* revenue amounts come to the actual amounts received, for the current year? (Note that we are not examining the budgeted amount for the forthcoming year, but the estimated amount for the present year). Because school board members (as well as administrators and some citizens) compare the proposed revenue amounts with the estimated, and only raise questions on those line items which differ significantly, you may want to know that these estimates are often made mid-year before all of the current year's revenue is received, making it necessary to revise the figures towards the end of the year. For this exercise you will need the material in Budgets A, B, & C and worksheet R-3, page 95.

Step 1: On your worksheet list a column for Estimated Revenue 1976-1977, a second column for Actual Revenue 1976-1977, and a column for the difference. Do this for two or more years depending on the data you have collected. On our worksheet item (N) the estimated total revenue for 1976-1977 came from Budget C, the budget for the 1978 fiscal year. Item (P) (from Budget B) is the actual amount received during the 1976-1977 year. It was obtained from the FY 79 budget summary.

Step 2: Item (Q) on the worksheet is the difference between the actual revenue and the estimated revenues ($20,661,998 − $19,839,-935 = $822,063). The actual revenue was $822,063 more than estimated.

Step 3: List each of the various sources of revenue and observe if, in successive years, there was a pattern of underestimating and/or overestimating the current year's estimated revenue.

Step 4: Find out why these over or underestimations exist. *Unlike* the differences between the budgeted revenue for forthcoming

Worksheet R—3

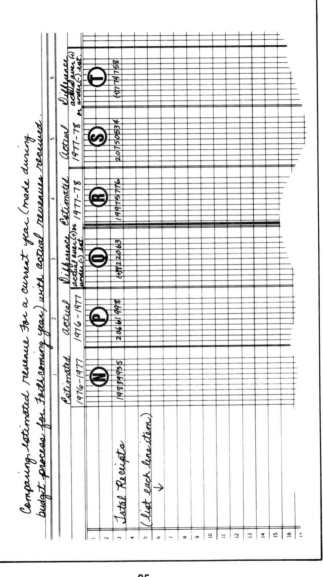

Comparing estimated revenue for a current year (made during budget process for forthcoming year) with actual revenue received.

	① Estimated 1976-1977	② Actual 1976-1977	③ Difference actual over(+) or under(-) est.	④ Estimated 1977-78	⑤ Actual 1977-78	⑥ Difference actual over(+) or under(-) est.
	ⓝ	ⓟ	ⓞ	ⓡ	ⓢ	ⓣ
Total Receipts	19,939,935	20,461,998	(+)522,063	19,975,776	20,750,534	(+)774,758
(List each line item) ↓						

BUDGET A
(FY 1980)

RECEIPTS

(September—June 30, 1978)

FROM LOCAL SOURCES	ACTUAL 1977-78	ESTIMATED 1978-79	BUDGETED 1979-80
Current Real Estate Taxes	$ 5,249,461.77	$ 6,725,059.00	$ 9,073,939.19
Public Utility Realty Tax	70,166.00	62,193.00	63,000.00
Current Per Capita Tax	196,233.79	185,000.00	185,000.00
Current Special Head Tax	392,467.39	370,000.00	370,000.00
Earned Income Tax	1,130,267.66	1,350,000.00	1,400,000.00
In Lieu of Taxes	26,380.67	27,597.00	27,600.00
Delinquent Taxes & Penalties	349,703.73	375,500.00	615,500.00
Tuition, Non-Residents	55,295.18	37,000.00	33,000.00
Interest on Investments	222,206.66	129,000.00	75,000.00
Rentals	100,689.75	136,000.00	174,000.00
Sale of Real Estate & Equipment	240.84	1,800.00	1,000.00
Miscellaneous Revenue	34,809.63	500.00	1,000.00
Total Local Sources	$ 7,827,923.07	$ 9,399,649.00	$12,019,039.19
Beginning Cash Balance Ⓛ	$ 1,607,209.70	$ 315,200.00	$ 265,282.00
TOTAL RECEIPTS Ⓢ	$20,750,534.76	$20,959,437.00	$23,344,926.19

years and the actual amounts received (which can sometimes be explained because a full year can bring significant changes through legislative action) these figures usually are compiled either midyear or later when a closer estimate should be possible. Some of the questions you might raise are: (1) Was the estimate correct at the time it was presented to the public and an unexpected windfall came to the district before June 30th (totaling $822,063)? (2) Was the estimate made deliberately low? Was the error unintended? Careless?

The Expenditure Analysis Worksheets
What you will be looking for:

In analyzing a line item budget (and some program budgets), you will want to determine which items or programs have had increases, and which have been decreased.

In addition, because you, as well as administrators and school board members, examine such proposed increases and decreases in the budget for the forthcoming year in comparison to the current year's expenses, you may want to review the past few years' budgets to see if the estimate of the current year's expenditures is fairly reliable. You will want to know if, in past years, the estimated expenditures came close to the actual expenditures recorded once the year was closed out. If not, you will want to note which particular expenditure estimates were way off.

You will then be able to observe if the estimated expenditures each year were accurate or inaccurate. More important, you will be able to observe if one particular category or line item of expenditures or income was consistently underestimated or overestimated. In some school districts expenditures in certain categories are overestimated by the administrators in order to suggest to the board that larger allocations are needed during the forthcoming year. In other instances, board members may direct administrators to include a high estimate for current teachers' salary expenses so that the figure proposed in the budget for the forthcoming year will appear to be low, thus enabling the board to enter or complete salary negotiations without revealing to the teachers' union just how much more the proposed budget has provided over current expenditure rates.

By comparing previous year's budgets with previous year's actual expenditures you can determine whether the budgeted figure means much in your school district. A school district's budget is supposed to be designed in advance to control expenditures; it is not a straight jacket.

Most states permit "budgetary transfers" or "modifications" which enable school board directors to change the exact amount of allocations during the year by transferring funds budgeted to one function or line item or program from another. Most states require that the school board (by majority or two-thirds vote) approve such transfer; a few states require that an amended budget be submitted to the state department of education/public instruction. Some school boards delegate to their superintendent the authority for such transfers; most school boards approve such transfers without fanfare, without debate, and often without any explanation.

Citizens seldom are informed about such transfers and almost never participate in this decision-making process. This is something else to look for as you examine the expenditures section of the budget.

When you have finished preparing your worksheets, you will want to use them to look for expenditures that have increased or decreased considerably in either dollar amount or percentage. You will want to look for questionable patterns of expenditures. And, of course, you will want to seek out explanations for such questionable patterns and apparent discrepancies which stick out like "sore thumbs."

Expenditure Worksheet E-1:
Which Items have been Increased or Decreased and How Much?

To make up this worksheet, (see page 100) you will need a copy of the proposed budget for the forthcoming year (usually available by March for public discussion if the board is to adopt it by June 30th). Be certain that it includes a column indicating the proposed budget amount for the forthcoming year, a column indicating the estimated expenditures for the present year, and a column indicating what the actual expenditures were for the year just ended.

Step 1: On your worksheet compare the line item or program on the left, along with the proposed budget amount in the first column and the estimated expenditure for the current year in the second column, as we have with items AA and BB from budget E. (Fy 80).

Step 2: Subtract the amounts in column 2 (the estimated expenditures) from the amount in column 1 and indicate the difference in column 3 showing whether the proposed amount is over (+) or under (−) the current estimated.

Step 3: In the 4th column figure, take the percentage difference between the proposed and the estimated amounts. To obtain this figure, divide the figure in column 3 by the figure in column 2. Carry it out to two places and you will have the percent increase or decrease. For the total budget, figure out, in the same way, the total percent increase in expenditures proposed.

$$
\begin{array}{r}
.019 = \text{rounded } .02 \text{ or } 2\% \\
191,270 \overline{)3,755.00} \\
191270 \\
\hline
173230 \\
172143 \\
\hline
10870
\end{array}
$$

Step 4: Circle the amounts in column 3 which represent somewhat large dollar increases (use a black pen) or decreases (use a red pen)—these may be considered the "sore thumbs." What constitutes a *large* dollar increase varies from community to community. In some, a large dollar variation might be $15,000—a sum which might pay for the salary of an additional teacher or counselor or provide sufficient funds for the field trips for the elementary grades which were dropped from the budget last year.

Step 5: Circle the percentages in column 4 which appear to be considerably larger or smaller than the percentage increase in the total budget. If the total budget was increased by 7%, a 10% increase or a 4% increase might be significant enough to circle.

Worksheet E—1

Identifying proposed increases or decreases in a budget for forth-coming year as compared to current year's estimated expenditure.

Item or Program	Proposed Budget 1979-80 (AA)	Estimated Expenditure 1975-77 (BB)	Difference Budget over (+) or under (-)	current year % difference
0112 Salaries, Bd. Admin.	195025	191270	+3755	2%
0151 Expenses, Admin.	32300	21950	+10350	32%
0211 Salaries, Principals	508000	500000	+8000	1%
0213 Salaries, Teachers	9314672	8792700	+521972	5%
0239 Other Expenses	52795	44667	+8128	15%
etc.				

BUDGETS E

FY80
EXPENDITURES

	Actual Expenditures 1977-78	Estimated Expenditures 1978-79	Budget 1979-1980
ADMINISTRATION			
0111 Salary, Board Stenographer (DD)(HH)	$ 2,160.00	(BB) $ 3,177.00	(AA) $ 3,000.
0112 Salaries, Educational Adm.	170,611.66	191,270.00	195,025.
0113 Salaries, Business Adm.	62,935.97	68,800.00	89,100.
0114 Salaries, Legal Services	13,499.72	13,500.00	13,500.
0115 Salaries, Tax Collection	37,239.26	35,800.00	43,400.
0121 Materials & Supplies, Adm.	8,334.91	9,980.00	11,500.
0125 Materials & Supplies, Tax Coll.	3,503.07	9,150.00	10,000.
0131 Expenses, Administration	27,098.57	21,950.00	32,300.

FY79
EXPENDITURES

	Estimated Expenditures 1977-78	Budget 1978-79
ADMINISTRATION		
0111 Salaries, Board Officials	(CC) $ 1,968.00	$ 2,496.00
0112 Salaries, Educational Adm.	176,200.00	190,970.00
0113 Salaries, Business Adm.	63,800.00	68,195.00
0114 Salaries, Legal Services	13,500.00	14,500.00
0115 Salaries, Tax Collection	37,500.00	40,225.00
0121 Materials & Supplies, Adm.	9,350.00	10,450.00
0125 Materials & Supplies, Tax Col.	8,000.00	8,000.00
0131 Expenses, Administration	28,350.00	29,300.00
0135 Expenses, Tax Collection	100.00	100.00
0151 Contracted Auditing Services	13,800.00	15,000.00
0154 Contracted Legal Services	5,500.00	6,000.00
0155 Contracted Tax Coll. Services	63,350.00	54,200.00
0159 Other Contracted Services	5,000.00	5,000.00
Total Administration	$ 426,418.00	444,436.00
INSTRUCTION		
0211 Salaries, Principals	$ 485,000.00	$ 514,600.00
0212 Salaries, Supervisors	328,000.00	336,053.00
0213 Salaries, Teachers	8,447,190.00	9,154,856.00

FY78
EXPENDITURES

	Actual Expenditures 1977-78	Estimated Expenditures 1978-79	Budget 1979-80
ADMINISTRATION			
0111 Salaries, Board Officials	$ 1,389.50	(EE) $ 1,248.00	(GG) $ 1,000.
0112 Salaries, Educational Adm.	170,079.61	169,115.00	176,700.
0113 Salaries, Business Adm.	54,369.75	57,500.00	63,800.
0114 Salaries, Legal Services	13,500.00	13,500.00	13,500.
0115 Salaries, Tax Collection	33,620.30	34,600.00	37,200.
0121 Materials and Supplies, Adm.	7,466.25	9,500.00	10,300.
0125 Materials & Supplies, Tax Collection	9,710.49	7,000.00	8,000.

Worksheet E—2

Reliability of "Estimated Expenditures." Comparing estimates (made during the budget process for forthcoming year) with actual expenditures for same year.

Item or Program	Estimated expenditures 1972-28 (CC)	Actual expenditures 1972-78 (DD)	Difference actual over(+) under(-)	Estimated expenditures 1976-77 (EE)	Actual expenditures 1976-77 (FF)	Difference actual over(+) under(-)
1						
2						
3 0111 Salary, Board	19680	21160	+192	1248	1296	+4800
4 0112 Salaries, Ed. Admin.	176200	1706.11	-5589	169115	1159817	-3298
5 0131 Expenses, Admin.						
6 etc.	28350	27098	-1252	35667	28164	-7506
7						
8 0211 Salaries, Principals	485000	483711	-1289	470000	459542	+195542
9 0213 Salaries, Teachers	8447110	8430138	-17052	8213500	7993498	-220002
10 0239 Other Expenses						
11 etc.	34871	32094	-2777	42400	39663	-2737
12						
13 0612 Salaries, Op.+Maint.						
14 etc.	18700000	18794432	+94432	19000000	18812827	-117173
15						
16						
17						

Step 6: Now you are ready to begin to raise some questions about the "sore thumbs." Why should the item "Expenses, Administration" increase by 32% while the "Principal's Salary" increased by 1% or 1.5%. Although the dollar increase for "Salaries, Teachers" is $521,972 it represents only a 5% increase. Is this sufficient to meet the mandated increments in teachers' salaries, the negotiated increases *and* the additional teachers needed to reduce grades 1-3 class sizes from 35 to 30 (a priority that the board and administration announced several months ago)? You will have any number of questions depending on your concerns or the degree to which the district's long-range plans are being met by this budget.

Caution—Before you get too wrapped up in comparing the proposed increases/decreases with the estimated amounts for the current year, you may want to determine if those estimated amounts are reliable (see Worksheet E-2), and also whether or not the proposed budget figure is strictly adhered to, or if "budgetary transfers" take place freely throughout the year (see worksheet E-3, page 106). Note that many of the same reasons cited during the Revenue discussion for underestimating or overestimating the various Revenue figures hold true for the *Expenditure* figures as well.

Expenditure Worksheet E-2:
How Reliable are the "Estimated Expenditure" Figures?

As indicated previously, the "Estimated Expenditures" for the current year are often the basis upon which proposed increases or decreases in the budget for the forthcoming year are measured. Because the proposed budget is prepared well before the end of the current year, the "Estimated Expenditures" may be no more than an educated guess (or a somewhat calculated under/overestimation). In order to determine whether or not you are wasting your time comparing the proposed budget with estimates that may not be too reliable, you may want to use Worksheet E-2 to help determine how reliable those figures were in the past.

Step 1: Obtain last year's budget plus the budgets for two years prior to that. Be certain that the budgets contain the usual three columns: Proposed or Adopted Budget, Estimated Expenditures, and Actual Expenditures (Budget E, page 101). If the "Actuals" are missing, obtain the figures from the school district's annual audit for that year or from the school financial report to the state.

Step 2: Prepare a worksheet (like the one on page 102) listing the name and number of the item or program to the left. List in column 1 the Estimated Expenditure for 1977–78, (item CC). List in column 2, the Actual Expenditures for 1977–78 (item DD). Do the same for other years.

Step 3: Find the difference between the "Estimated" and the "Actuals" by subtracting the lower number from the higher and enter the amount in column 3. Be certain to indicate if the "Actual" is over (+) or under (−) the "Estimated."

Step 4: Look for the questionable patterns. Does it appear that the "Estimated Expenditures" are always higher than the "Actual," as is the case on our worksheet? Or, to put it another way, are the figures on the current year's estimated expenses overestimated fairly consistently?

Step 5: Now you are ready to begin to raise some questions about the proposed budget and/or the previous budgets. If you find that the "Salaries, Teachers" category always has been overestimated, you may want to find out if this is done in order to give the board "hidden flexibility" for collective bargaining purposes. You may observe from your figures on Budget Comparison Worksheet E-1 that the FY 80 proposed budget 1979–80 provides for a 5% increase on this line item. (You do not know, however whether there will be more or fewer teachers on the payroll.) However, if the "Estimated Figure" given for 1978–79 is revised downward in order to bring it into line with what might be expected as a lower "Actual" expenditure, the proposed budget actually may be providing more than a 5% increase.

Similarly on "Salaries, Administration." Although there is far less reason to be off at all in "estimating" the current year's amount in this category (substitutes are not hired in case of administrators' absence, nor are new administrators unexpectedly hired, even though occasionally some may leave just before the end of the year), if the "estimated" 1978-79 figure were revised downward by $3000-$5000, then the proposed budget increase (as identified on Worksheet E-1) would total approximately $7000-$9000 or a percentage increase of 4% or 5% as opposed to the 2% shown.

Caution: Again, before you get too excited about a high or low degree of reliability in the "estimated" figures, you may want to determine whether or not the adopted budget figures are usually strictly adhered to in all or only some categories and line items (see Worksheet E-3, page 106).

Expenditure Worksheet E-3:
How Closely Has the Budget Been Followed?

Is the budget, once adopted, strictly adhered to, considered a relatively loose guide, or freely exceeded in some line items and adhered to in other line items or programs?

As indicated previously, in some school districts "Budgetary Transfers" or "Modifications" are so widespread that it hardly pays to get excited about the proposed budget—unless you are prepared to press for some closer budgetary control. By reviewing several budgets of previous years along with the "Actual Expenditures" for the same years, you may get some idea about where your school district stands on this issue.

Step 1: Obtain the most recent "Actual Expenditures" figures available along with the budget as adopted for that same year. Then obtain at least two additional budgets and "Actuals" for the preceding years. (You may already have this information if you obtained it for Worksheet E-2.) The district's annual audit usually will contain both the adopted budget and the actual expenditures for each year.

Worksheet E—3

Identifying consistency of budgeted expenditure for previous year with actual expenditure for the same year.

Item or Program	Budget 1977-79	Actual 1977-79	Difference actually over (+) or under (-) budget	%	Budget 1976-77	Actual 1976-77	Difference actually over (+) under (-) budget	%
Travel Expenses	10000	15000	+5000	+50%				
Teachers Salaries	10000000	9000000	-1000000	-10%				
Examples from sample budgets:								
0112 Salaries Ed Admin	176700	170611	-6089	-3.5%	144500	159117	15117	10%
0121 Expenses, Admin								
etc.								
0211 Salaries, Principals	503000	270918	+4902	-1.8%	346650	341161	6489	2.3%
0212 Salaries, Teachers	6511745	6493013S	-14169	-3.9%	496750	499592	-7268	1.4%
239 Other Expenses		14430138	-3598540	-4.5%	8195750	7993996	-202052	2.5%
etc.	532150	32094	-21156	-65%	5304%	3463	134953	3.3%
0112 Salaries per Maint	1993026	1959952	-33094	-2.7%	2001996	1852527	-149169	6.5%
etc.								

Step 2: Prepare a worksheet listing the name of the line item or program on the left. List in column 1 the adopted budget figure for the 1977–78 budget, taken from the FY 78 budget (page 101) (GG on Worksheet E–3). In column 2 list the "Actual Expenditures" for 1977–1978 found on the FY 80 budget (page 101) (DD on Worksheet E–3). Do the same for the other years.

Step 3: Find the difference between the budget figure and the actual figure by subtracting the lower number from the higher number and enter the figure in column 3, indicating if the "Actual Expenditure" was over (+) or under (−) the budget.

Step 4: In column 4, figure out the percent difference between the actual and the budget figures. (Illustrated on page 99.) To do this, divide your figure in column 3 by the amount in column 2. Carry it out to two places and you will have the percent difference between the Actual and the Budget figures.

Step 5: Observe the amounts in columns 3 and 4 for each year for which you have figures to see if any "sore thumbs" or questionable patterns are noticeable. For example: do you note that every year the Actual Teachers Salaries are under the budgeted amount, while "Expenses, Operations and Maintenance" is considerably over the budget?

Step 6: Now you are ready to begin to examine some of the questionable patterns emerging. In fact if there appear to be wide variations every year—even though in different directions—you may have reasons to question the degree to which any budgetary control is exerted. If, however, there are particular items which are consistently and considerably overspent (that is, the Actual Expenditures are high on the plus (+) side in columns 3 and 4) or other items consistently underspent, you may want to question whether this is an unwritten policy, a hidden flexibility built into the budget, an oversight by the program budget manager, or what.

Caution: Again, you may have to remind yourself not to become hypnotized by the figures. Unfortunately, budgets which present line items alone do not encourage your understanding of what the figures mean to the program or to the children. As more states begin to require program budgets or more school districts themselves begin to prepare their budgets first on a program basis and then translate it into line item to conform to their state's reporting system, you will find it much easier to relate the budget figures to the programs.

Additional Analyses of Expenditures

Per Pupil Expenditures: In addition to analyzing the increases and/or decreases in expenditures, you may wish to do a more detailed analysis of your school district's expenditures on a per-pupil basis. Find out from your school or state officials if "Average Daily Attendance" or "Average Daily Membership" is the standard measure which constitutes the pupil count in your state. Then divide the total expenditures by the number of pupils expressed as ADA or ADM in order to obtain the average expenditure per pupil. For instance, a school district with a budget of $30,000,000 and an Average Daily Attendence of 15,000 spends an average of $2,000 per pupil (ADA).

In order to determine what is being spent per pupil (ADA) for a particular school within your school district (if your central administration school district does not have totals by schools), you will have to obtain either from the board minutes, or from salary schedules and personnel assignments, the total salaries being paid to the personnel assigned to that building. Reviewing the district's purchase orders and supply flow charts may provide you with specific information on the total cost of supplies coming into your school. Some costs, such as general administration and maintenance, will have to be apportioned equally throughout the school district on a per-pupil basis. If this type of analysis shows a considerable discrepancy between expenditures per pupil in one school as compared to another or to the district-wide average expenditure, you will want to seek some explanations. An analysis by Ellen Lurie shows this can be done (Illustrations 25 and 26, pages 114 and 115).

A number of school districts include in their budget an analysis of costs per pupil broken down according to kindergarten, elementary, intermediate or junior high schools, and senior high schools. You can then examine the figures for several years to see if the expenditures in one category are exceeding costs in another (see "Analysis of Cost Per Pupil," Illustration 27, page 116).

Personnel Cost Analysis: Many budgets list not only a total amount budgeted for various salaries, but also the exact number of persons included in each category. You can then examine the current and previous budgets to note the changes in the number of personnel from year to year, as well as the average salary changes within the various categories given (see Edina, Minnesota, Budget 1975–1976 and Fairfax County Public Schools, School Board's Approved Budgets for the School and Fiscal Year ending June 30, 1978 (Illustration 28, page 117).

Comparing your School Budget Figures with Other Districts

You may want to compare the specific revenues and expenditures of your school district to that of other school districts, to state-wide averages, to national averages. You also may wish to compare the teachers' salaries, various fringe benefit costs, expenditures for textbooks, debt interest, revenue sources and myriad additional factors. Although school board and teacher associations regularly do such comparisons during or before negotiating a new contrct, it is very helpful if the community does its own research on all issues in order to understand the actual budget implications.

Expenditures Per Pupil: In order to compare the income or expenditure figures of your school district to other school districts within your state, you will need to obtain the annual state-wide statistical report on school district financial details. Virtually every state publishes such an annual report which lists income and expenditure figures school district by school district. Many of the state publications list expenditures by functional category (Administration, Instruction, Operation and Maintenance, etc.) in addition to total expenditures. A number of states also list district-by-district expenditures within those functional categories on a per-pupil basis. If per-pupil figures are not given in your state publication, you will have to construct your own by obtaining a listing from state department of education/public instruction, of the Average Daily

Attendance (ADA) or Average Daily Membership (ADM) for each school district (Illustration 29, pages 119 through 121).

If your state publication lists the Midcity School District's expenditure for Maintenance as $3,000,000 and the ADM is 30,000, you can easily divide the $3,000,000 by 30,000 and discover that the per-pupil* (ADM) expenditure for Maintenance is $100. If the expenditure for Maintenance for Suburbia School District is $2,000,000 and the ADM is 32,000, $62.50 is the per pupil expenditure (ADM) for Maintenance.

You will not necessarily begin to raise questions on these facts alone even though Midcity School District is spending 50% more per pupil on Maintenance than Surburbia School District. If, however, you discover that Center City School District, Other City School District, and Any City School District all spend between $74.20 and $83.40 per pupil (ADM) for Maintenance, you will want to find out why your school district is spending $100 per pupil. It is important to compare your school district's expenditures to districts of similar size and similar characteristics. The number of pupils, expressed in average daily membership (ADM) or average daily attendence (ADA) or any other designation your state Department of Education/Public Instruction utilizes, is a matter of public record and is readily available to you from the state. But characteristics other than pupil enrollment are not so readily available. You will want to know which of the schools with comparable pupil counts are urban, suburban, rural, or consolidated, and which of the districts is most like yours in terms of type and ages of buildings. You will want to know locations—a district on the opposite side of the state may differ in many respects from yours.

If you are uncertain of which schools are generally comparable to yours a good source of information is your own school superintendent or officials from the county, regional or intermediate school offices. Note carefully the basis on which they select particular schools.

Once you have your statistics from the state and the names of several comparable school districts, you are ready to make another worksheet to study the comparative figures.

---

* "Per pupil" is a shorthand term which means per pupil as calculated on an average daily enrollment or average daily attendance basis.

Budget Comparison Worksheet C-1:
How Do the Expenditures Per Pupil in your School District Compare to the Expenditures in Other School Districts?

Step 1: Obtain from your state department of education, or state superintendent of public instruction, your state's most recent annual statewide statistical report on school district financial details (Illustrations 20 and 29, pages 62, 119 through 121).

Step 2: Find out (from your school officials, from county or regional school officials, or from state officials) which district is comparable to yours.

Step 3: Prepare a worksheet. In the left-hand column list the various functional categories for which per-pupil expenditures are available (Administration, Instruction, etc.). Along the top columns list your school district, the state average, your county average, and a similar district average (a figure which you will probably have to derive yourself). Also list separately each of the similar districts for comparison.

Step 4: Copy all the figures for each school district on your worksheet. Also copy the state average (usually found at the beginning or end of the individual school districts' listing), and your county or regional average, if given.

Step 5: Figure out the average for similar school districts in each of the functional categories. On our worksheet, line 1 ("Administration") figures in column 7 (Allentown), column 8 (Lancaster), column 9 (York), etc. were added together (27.69 + 41.95 + 54.34...) and the total divided by 7, because there were seven similar cities. This gives an average of 42.71. Then proceed to line 2, "Instruction", then to line 3, etc.

Step 6: Examine the figures and circle those from your school district that are significantly over or under the similar district average. In the worksheet, the figure for Reading's Administration is under, while Operation and Maintenance of Plant is over. In addition, "Fixed Charges" is also somewhat over.

Worksheet C—1

Comparing per-pupil (ADM) expenditures for selected functions with state, county and similar school district average expenditures.

	1 Reading School district	2	3 State average	4 County average	5 Similar district average*
1 Administration	2796		4253	4184	4271
2 Instruction	77047		69904	67927	76439
3 Pupil Personnel Serv.	3055		3107	2436	3896
4 Op. and Maint. of Plant	21819		14281	14098	15544
5 Fixed Charges	12003		9718	9075	9808
6 Others	5585		8693	7092	8160
7 Current Expenditures	122243		109956	104813	118119
8 Total Expenditures	139189		126988	124598	131506
9					
10 Source: Our Schools Today "Public School Financial					
11 Statistics Report 1973-74" Vol. 14 No. 7					
12 Pennsylvania Department of Education 1975					
13					
14 *average of columns #7-14					
15					
16					
17					

Comparing per pupil (Average Daily Membership) expenditures for Reading School District with state, county and similar school district expenditures for selected functions.

Step 7: Now you are ready to start raising some questions. Is your district's per-pupil expenditure on Administration low because you are understaffed or underpaid? Or is it because some expenses which should be reported as Administration are being reported as Instruction? Are the expenditures for Operations and Maintenance of Plant so much higher for Reading than for the district average because Reading's buildings are newer or older, because the custodians are paid salaries far exceeding those in similar cities, or because the patronage system is based in the school district's operation/maintenance department?

Worksheet C—1 — (Continued)

	6		7		8		9		10		11		12	

Allentown	Lancaster	York	Bethlehem	Scranton	Harrisburg	Easton
2769	4195	5434	3226	3186	6144	4948
64713	81252	92454	68668	73450	89599	64937
3348	4683	5107	3268	1857	6008	3003
14089	18660	16462	15292	15627	15133	13556
8236	9726	12911	9567	6355	13460	8400
6338	7012	7534	5519	7478	16032	8222
99493	125518	139892	105540	107954	145375	103067
108841	135978	164566	122984	118391	153557	116224

Step 8: You may want to make additional worksheets for previous years to see if your school district's per-pupil expenditures in any one particular area are always higher or lower than similar districts.

Teachers' Salaries and Administrators' Salaries In Other Districts

Since one of the major school budget items in every school district is professional salaries, you may wish to compare teachers' or administrators' or other specialists' salaries with those in other school districts. You also may want to look at the comparative costs of fringe

Illustration No. 25
COMPARING SCHOOL BY SCHOOL EXPENDITURES

December 18, 1971

TO: PARENTS, STUDENTS, AND OTHERS CONCERNED ABOUT HIGH SCHOOLS

FROM: Ellen Lurie

SUBJECT: High School Profiles

As you know we have been trying for over a year to obtain high school data
on costs, teacher salaries, reading scores, etc. Last Tuesday evening
at the public Board of Education meeting, Chancellor Scribner ordered that
one copy of the October 1971 High School Profiles be placed in the third
floor library at headquarters. It is there now. He has promised that
quantities will be distributed next month, but since that promise has been
made repeatedly, don't count on it.

In the meantime, a high official lent us the report, probably to keep us
from speaking about it so often. United Bronx Parents has been good enough
to xerox several copies. These are now available at UBP, Equal, Harlem Parents Union and Queens Lay Advocate Service.

EQUAL has called a meeting for January 5, at 7 P.M. at the New York Civil
Liberties Union, 84 Fifth Avenue to analyze this material and to plan further action. You are welcome to attend this session if you can. At the
first opportunity, we will want to prepare a full summary and distribute
it to parent associations, student groups, and community organizations.

However, I personally feel burdened by the possession of this booklet,
which I must return in two days to the "source" at headquarters. Therefore, I thought I would make some brief notes available to all of you
immediately. I think I have copied the data correctly, but please accept
this as a rough preliminary summary. When we meet in January, we can prepare
a more thorough report.

Attached you will find:

a. My brief summary and some tables which I have developed
   highlighting some of the material in the Profiles

b. Copies of two appendices from the Report which were
   duplicated by United Bronx Parents

c. Sample profile sheets for two high schools, also duplicated
   by United Bronx Parents.

The information is overwhelming in its implications. I only hope that our
sense of indignation has not been dulled and that we find the energy and
strength to work together to make effective use of this data which we have
all tried so long to obtain.

Illustration No. 26
DOLLARS PER PUPIL BY SCHOOL

ACADEMIC HIGH SCHOOLS GETTING THE MOST AND THE LEAST MONEY PER STUDENT

(1970-1971 budget, tax levy funds only, not including custodial service)

THE LEAST

SCHOOL	DOLLARS PER PUPIL	PERCENT WHITE	UTILI- ZATION	PERCENT RETARDED TWO YRS OR MORE IN READING
Benjamin Franklin	$ 605	3.3%	177%	51.4%
John Jay	$ 625	43.1%	171%	59.0%
Boys High	$ 637	0.7%	115%	48.0%
Dewitt Clinton	$ 642	33.5%	150%	48.1%
Thomas Jefferson	$ 656	6.1%	152%	54.2%
Morris	$ 673	0.7%	188%	45.1%
Ft. Hamilton	$ 677	76.5%	146%	24.9%
Eastern District	$ 679	8.3%	140%	49.3%
Brandeis	$ 689	5.7%	165%	60.9%
F. K. Lane	$ 709	24.4%	114%	49.0%

THE MOST

Music & Art	$1073	62.9%	85%	2.6%

VOCATIONAL HIGH SCHOOLS GETTING THE MOST AND THE LEAST MONEY PER STUDENT

SCHOOL	DOLLARS PER PUPIL	PERCENT WHITE	UTILIZ- ATION	PERCENT RETARDED TWO YRS OR MORE IN READING

THE LEAST

Cent. Commercial	$937	7.8%	132%	24.6%
Maxwell	$1001	33.7%	167%	49.0%

Excerpt from Ellen Lurie's analysis of dollars per pupil budgeted for New York High Schools.

Illustration No. 27
ANALYSIS OF COST PER PUPIL

MONTGOMERY COUNTY (MD)
ANALYSIS OF COST PER PUPIL

	Kindergarten	Grades 1-6	Grades 7-12	Total K-12
Fiscal 1973 Actual				
Expenditures	$6,577,724	$67,603,986	$86,050,753	$160,232,463
Pupils 9/30/72	8,406	57,411	60,494	126,311
Cost Per Pupil	$ 783	$ 1,178	$ 1,422	$ 1,269
Fiscal 1974 Actual				
Expenditures	$6,904,564	$71,060,474	$94,063,107	$172,028,145
Pupils 9/28/73	8,295	55,980	61,214	125,489
Cost Per Pupil	$ 832	$ 1,269	$ 1,537	$ 1,371
Fiscal 1975 Budget				
Expenditures (Budget)	$7,865,681	$78,310,760	$105,175,703	$191,352,144
Pupils 9/30/74 (Actual)	8,502	54,115	61,014	123,631
Cost Per Pupil	$ 925	$ 1,447	$ 1,724	$ 1,548
Fiscal 1976 Request				
Expenditures	$9,162,694	$90,174,131	$118,808,785	$218,145,610
Pupils 9/30/75	8,493	53,085	60,873	122,451
Cost Per Pupil	$ 1,079	$ 1,699	$ 1,952	$ 1,781

Note: Summer School, programs financed through federal, state or private agency grants and revolving and management accounts are excluded from cost of regular day school operations.

	Included	Excluded	Grand Total
Fiscal 1973	$160,232,463	$14,588,885	$174,821,348
Fiscal 1974	172,028,145	15,631,677	187,659,822
Fiscal 1975	191,352,144	20,247,638	211,599,782
Fiscal 1976	218,145,610	23,562,574	241,708,184

H-1

Montgomery County Public Schools Budget FY 76

benefits (insurance, sick days, preparation time); these also may be significant items. There are a number of sources for this information—and you should be keenly aware of a number of problems in trying to make legitimate comparisons.

Sources: Almost every state department of education or department of public instruction requires local school boards to fill out a form at the

Illustration No. 28
ANALYZING PERSONNEL COSTS

AS OF 7/01/77   **FAIRFAX COUNTY PUBLIC SCHOOL SYSTEM**
1977-78 PERSONNEL COMPLEMENT SUMMARY
FUND—SCHOOL OPERATING FUND NO. 04

$ IN THOUSANDS—PERSONNEL ACTUAL.

PROG NO-F1981

NO.	OBJECT— DESCRIPTION	1975 ACTUAL AMOUNT	PERS.	1976 ACTUAL AMOUNT	PERS.	1977 ESTIMATED AMOUNT	PERS.	1978 SUPT BUDGET AMOUNT	PERS.	1978 APPROVED BUDGET AMOUNT	PERS.
110	PROFESSIONAL	$3,750.9	178.0	$4,688.3	199.0	$4,833.7	186.8	$4,820.0	179.5	$ 5,249.1	189.0
110A	COORDINATOR	313.1	24.0	415.9	21.0	329.8	15.0	328.0	13.5	341.7	13.5
110B	GUID DIRECTOR	682.5	40.0	774.0	40.0	822.5	40.0	921.1	40.0	970.8	40.0
110C	PSYCHOLOGIST	586.8	35.0	793.0	43.0	941.4	53.0	1,123.2	58.0	1,261.3	63.0
110F	SUPERVISOR	326.4	18.0	351.2	18.0	353.1	16.0	368.6	17.0	393.7	17.0
110G	DIRECTOR	178.5	7.0	220.1	8.0	231.4	8.0	230.8	8.0	242.7	8.0
110I	SUPERINTENDENT	115.5	3.0	125.6	3.0	127.7	3.0	127.7	3.0	137.5	3.0
110J	EDP COORDINATOR	24.4	1.0	27.3	1.0	28.4	1.0	29.8	1.0	25.9	1.0
	ACCRUAL TOTAL	109.1		107.4		151.2		181.2		181.4	
	OBJECT TOTAL	$6,087.2	306.0	$7,502.8	333.0	$7,819.2	322.8	$ 8,130.3	320.0	$ 8,804.0	334.5
111	PRINCIPAL	$7,220.4	344.0	$8,035.1	343.0	$8,259.7	345.0	$ 8,376.2	343.0	$8,853.8	343.0
111B	ASST PRIN	.0		90.8	4.0	111.3	4.0	113.2	4.0	119.3	4.0
	ACCRUAL TOTAL	422.1		443.0		477.7		537.7			
	OBJECT TOTAL	$7,642.5	344.0	$8,568.9	347.0	$8,848.7	349.0	$ 9,027.1	347.0	$ 9,481.5	347.0
113	SPEC ED TEACHER	$ 169.9	18.0	$297.1	26.0	$ 305.2	27.0	$ 2,688.4	220.0	$ 2,736.9	216.0
113A	MOD RTD TCHR	198.7	22.0	230.9	25.0	243.2	24.0	234.5	20.0	244.9	20.0
113B	MILDLY RTD TCHR	740.2	77.0	853.3	78.0	781.8	70.0	736.3	59.0	767.1	58.0
113C	PHY HAND TCHR	158.1	18.5	161.8	16.0	194.9	21.0	277.4	24.0	284.3	23.0
113D	SPEECH THERAPST	855.5	75.0	1,015.7	94.0	1,083.9	94.0	1,146.8	95.0	1,177.2	93.0
113E	VIS HAND TCHR	76.6	9.0	95.1	10.0	116.5	10.0	123.0	10.0	129.6	10.0
113F	LEARN DIS TCHR	1,873.3	187.0	2,905.9	255.0	3,472.0	281.0	1,275.4	114.5	1,610.5	114.5
113G	HEARING TCHR	288.4	33.0	503.1	47.0	610.9	55.0	726.0	58.0	706.4	55.0
113H	EM DISB TCHR	162.9	13.0	406.3	39.0	533.6	47.0	719.5	59.0	734.5	57.0
113I	MULT HANDICAP	117.7	14.0	106.0	11.0	128.2	12.0	133.8	12.0	141.9	12.0
113J	VOC TEACHER	54.0	7.0	129.1	10.0	172.6	13.0	193.1	13.0	235.3	17.0
113K	PRE SCHOOL TCHR	95.1	17.0	407.0	45.0	596.1	61.0	698.2	61.0	719.8	61.0
113M	MUSIC THERAPIST	30.1	3.0	.0		.0		.0		.0	
113R	PLACEMENT SPEC	42.6	2.0	24.1	2.0	38.7	2.0	40.0	2.0	42.2	2.0
	ACCRUAL TOTAL	606.7		908.7		1,341.3		1,668.9		1,595.1	
	OBJECT TOTAL	$5,469.9	495.5	$8,043.9	658.0	$9,618.9	717.0	$10,661.3	747.5	$11,125.9	738.5
114	SPECIAL TCHR	$1,219.2	123.0	$1,678.4	153.0	$1,970.2	128.7	$ 1,675.7	120.5	$ 2,272.8	161.6
114A	STRING & BAND	817.7	60.0	759.8	63.0	842.4	63.0	840.6	63.0	716.1	47.0
114C	READING TCHR	1,785.2	146.5	2,106.3	152.0	2,207.5	153.5	2,274.3	154.0	2,393.0	164.0
114D	LIBRARIAN	2,610.6	209.5	2,952.4	209.5	3,013.0	204.5	3,117.3	204.5	3,267.6	203.5
114E	HEAD START TCHR	156.2	16.0	201.0	16.0	209.5	16.0	241.0	16.0	241.6	16.5
114F	TITLE I TCHR	710.3	63.0	862.8	69.5	835.3	62.0	993.5	65.5	990.6	65.5
114G	GUIDANCE COUN	2,971.1	215.0	3,347.5	215.5	3,446.5	214.0	3,544.2	211.0	3,781.9	214.0
114H	COMP ED TEACHER	67.6	4.0	86.7	8.0	71.4	5.0	66.5	5.0	182.8	15.0
114I	VOC TEACHER	1,362.4	109.0	325.8	22.0	2,061.8	129.7	2,153.3	129.2	2,300.1	129.3
114K	DRIVER ED TCHR	166.8	11.0	179.9	11.0	190.4	11.0	185.0	11.0	195.8	11.0
114L	VISITING TCHR	300.0	22.0	402.8	30.0	653.9	49.5	731.9	51.0	789.5	51.0
114N	MEDIA SPEC	120.5	6.0	107.9	5.0	48.4	2.0	59.1	3.0	62.3	3.0
114P	HUMAN REL COUN	221.7	20.0	276.8	19.0	154.3	10.0	160.7	10.0	161.8	10.0
114S	PHY/OCCUP THERP	4.6	.5	97.3	10.5	138.9	12.0	148.9	12.0	155.6	12.0
114V	VOC TEACHER	.0		.0		.0		32.1	3.0	.0	

(Ill. No. 28—continued on next page)

Budget detail to assist in analyzing personnel costs.
Fairfax County Public School System Budget 1978.

beginning of the year detailing *each and every* professional on the payroll along with their salaries, years of service, certification, etc. Most state education departments then summarize this information and publish it. (Illustration 30, page 126). In addition, some states summarize similar information on a per-pupil basis (as does Minnesota, which lists "Instructional Salaries per pupil" as one of the items analyzed on a school district by school district basis, Illustration 29, pages 119 through 121).

Illustration No. 28—(Continued)

PERSONNEL COST ANALYSIS
FOR 1975-76 BUDGET

	DISTRICT-WIDE Certificated Personnel Costs	1974-75 Budget	75-76 Budget Advanced on 74-75 Sched.	Comments
(210.5)	005 000 000 102 District Coordinators			
	Dist. Curriculum Coord. (1)	$19,720	$24,200	74-75 sal. $24,200; $4480 in CQE program 005 430 120 104. Program elim.
	Coord. of Vocational Ed. (1)	19,400	18,900	75-76. 74-75 sal. $24,900; $6000 in Community Service, 005 940 946 102.
		39,120	43,100	
(210.32)	005 121 000 114 Elem. Classroom Teach., Instrumental Music (3)	—	50,800	Transferred from building codes
(210.32)	005 189 000 114 Classroom Teachers, Handicapped			
	Speech Therapists, 1974-75 (5)	74,150		
	Speech Therapists, 1975-76 (5)		75,500	
(210.5)	005 522 000 106 Elem. Inst. Assts. Two half-time, one full time, 1974-75 (2) 1975-76 (2)	39,350	39,600	
(210.5)	005 522 000 110 Asst. to Cluster Prin. (1)	25,300	—	Position eliminated 1975-76
(210.32)	005 522 000 165 Sabbatical Leaves, Elementary Teachers Teachers (3) .... Teachers (2)	18,976	21,544	
(210.32)	005 522 720 106 Elem. Art Consult. (1)	21,083	21,083	
(210.12)	005 522 860 165 Sabbatical Leaves, Elem. Principals Principals (0)	—	—	
(210.32)	005 522 890 114 Elem. Alternatives Program Teachers (2)	38,350	23,550	Savings by replacements. 74-75 personnel transferred to buildings.

Personnel Cost Analysis—Edina, Minnesota

Illustration No. 29

COMPARATIVE FIGURES AMONG DISTRICTS

DEVELOPMENT REGIONS, COUNTIES, AND SCHOOL DISTRICTS	% RCPT FED	% RCPT STATE	ADM-N	INS SAL R	OTH INS LER	TRANS	ATT HND	POP LAB PERT	PLM AINT	FIX CHG OED	FOD SERV	STU ACT DIV	TRFRS	COM SER RV	CAP OUT LAY	DS BR AR	AMEN ITIES	TOTAL EXP	STATE & LOC & OPER COSTS	BOND-ED DEBT	1975 EARC VALUE	1975 INCOME	STATE & LOC 1976 EFFEC COSTS
NOBLES CO.																							
ADRIAN	7	58	43	624	12	86	8	93	11	64	67	31	49	6	139	28	3	1,363	968	81	20,687	9,984	936
BREWSTER	7	51	62	562	95	81	11	95	15	54	75	4	31	44	67	59	0	1,284	883	523	22,465	9,984	863
ELLSWORTH	7	51	80	559	106	82	1	101	17	62	82	51	22	0	104	39	0	1,305	921		23,506	10,187	911
ROUND LAKE	3	55	105	632	53	118		197	29	46	70	0	17	15	67	66	0	1,355	967	5	24,946	19,201	929
WORTHINGTON	3	56	49	787	172	62	10	86	26	65	58	8	4	26	29	41	9	1,437	1,152	318	17,137	17,292	1,117
PIPESTONE CO.																							
EDGERTON	12	40	105	722	143	245	7	176	52	96	80	0	4	109	1,751	183	47	3,718	1,184	1,791	37,479	22,978	1,153
JASPER	8	49	56	630	73	88	4	94	15	42	68	45	45	2	17	73	1	1,252	932	720	22,389	13,395	907
PIPESTONE	6	68	30	689	123	74	12	102	18	47	59	32	3	67	76	120	17	1,470	1,014	1,013	14,047	13,934	991
RUTHTON	10	54	73	662	103	95	2	113	14	54	90	44	160	1	41	65	17	1,518	1,062	499	16,235	7,616	1,022
REDWOOD CO.																							
BELVIEW	5	66	95	648	79	102	0	68	38	64	60	26	66	6	77	74	1	1,405	1,033	428	24,240	12,839	1,000
LAMBERTON	6	41	64	695	59	71	4	91	13	67	67	60	40	5	93	147	0	1,387	951	1,212	21,658	14,176	927
MILROY	6	41	88	639	73	95	0	84	13	37	68	25	14	5	35	98	0	1,485	1,028	890	33,729	17,794	1,018
MORGAN	5	43	85	618	108	91	5	84	14	53	60	21	68	37	64	71	0	1,452	1,038	368	33,728	17,137	997
REDWOOD FALLS	4	62	44	627	101	55	5	74	12	24	52	38	51	39	39	64	0	1,216	922	142	14,815	14,792	908
SANBORN	5	52	62	707	95	102	6	92	24	52	59	2	7	0	83	83	6	1,426	1,094	523	23,386	14,815	781
WABASSO	7	50	47	749	105	109	3	92	10	24	59	0	13	0	64	64	0	1,305	1,090		21,095	10,955	1,070
WALNUT GROVE	8	47	74	612	83	83	0	86	9	51	77	0	100	0	55	56	8	1,321	933		28,226	14,420	893
ROCK CO.																							
HILLS—BEAVER CRE	4	55	74	585	129	84	0	101	44	73	65	62	44	21	131	21	0	1,437	1,012	161	21,044	11,955	988
LUVERNE	4	59	39	555	103	55	7	92	7	47	60	61	61	1	266	29	1	1,393	849	593	21,090	11,940	840
MAGNOLIA	5	41	144	668	157	82	1	139	18	44	93	44	3	0	55			1,477	1,164	200	34,074	11,448	1,101

Excerpts from UPDATE, SPECIAL REPORT SUMMER, 1977.

Per Pupil Expenditures and other comparative figures for each Minnesota School District. Minnesota Department of Education, 1977

(Ill. No. 29—continued on next page)

Illustration No. 29—(Continued)

DEVELOPMENT REGIONS, COUNTIES, AND SCHOOL DISTRICTS	DISTRICT ENROLLMENTS			TOTAL PUPIL UNITS 1975-6	ENROLLS %	PUPIL DATA				PROFESSIONAL STAFFING			MILL RATES	
	KGN	ELEM GR1-6	SEC GR7-12			% HCPD	% NON-WITE	% ATT-NDCE	% TRAN	TOTAL STAFF FTE	PUPIL TOTAL /FTE	AVG SALE /FTE	NON-AGRIC	EARC
REGION 07E CHISAGO CO														
CHISAGO CO														
CHISAGO LAKES	155	865	1,081	2,465	101	0.5	0.9	93.9	100.6	114	18.5	10,772	65.91	44.01
NORTH BRANCH	160	991	1,079	2,523	100	1.2	1.7	93.9	101.3	110	20.0	11,200	77.26	51.97
RUSH CITY	73	401	490	1,093	99	0.1	1.7	94.6	80.0	53	17.7	11,734	57.76	37.24
TAYLORS FALLS	27	176	258	550	99	0.0	0.7	95.0	80.4	30	15.5	10,237	55.72	36.07
ISANTI CO														
BRAHAM	81	481	597	1,419	94	0.5	0.4	94.2	99.3	65	18.6	11,372	70.77	45.10
CAMBRIDGE	285	1,649	2,085	4,623	101	8.1	1.1	94.0	74.8	223	17.7	11,285	68.95	48.67
KANABEC CO														
MORA	110	794	936	2,147	98	2.6	0.6	94.7	82.5	97	19.1	11,035	55.53	34.72
OGILVIE	69	297	334	799	103	0.7	1.4	93.6	91.5	40	17.1	11,058	70.02	37.55
MILLE LACS CO														
ISLE	29	212	300	653	103	2.4	4.4	94.1	92.9	37	14.8	11,546	52.98	31.78
MILACA	168	794	1,135	2,336	92	1.6	1.9	93.9	84.7	110	18.2	11,318	64.20	43.63
ONAMIA	68	431			91	1.3	13.0	93.1	102.5	67	16.9	10,707	63.43	41.81
PRINCETON	187	1,202	1,330	3,076	101	1.9	1.9	95.8	95.0	153	17.4	13,315	65.78	45.16
PINE CO														
ASKOV	32	196	244	566	94	0.0	3.8	95.0	97.3	31	15.6	12,181	85.44	48.67
FINLAYSON	14	115	131	293	102	1.5	0.8	95.3	95.7	17	15.1	10,545	60.56	33.90
HINCKLEY	69	388	489	1,105	98	0.6	4.8	94.4	88.0	50	18.9	11,568	63.82	43.24
PINE CITY	110	571	889	1,899	101	2.0	0.4	93.8	88.2	90	18.6		65.44	42.12
SANDSTONE	50	348	277	666	92	4.0	0.9	93.7	75.7	43	16.6	11,274	47.13	28.12
WILLOW RIVER	33	223			94	0.2	1.7	92.4	95.8	37	15.4	11,123	63.04	34.60

Illustration No. 29—*(Continued)*

Special Report

Vol. 11, Special Edition No. 2   Summer 1977   MINNESOTA DEPARTMENT OF EDUCATION

1975–76 School District Comparisons

With this publication the State Department of Education issues its fourth annual report on statistics characterizing Minnesota school districts which operate both elementary and secondary schools.

As in previous years, the pupil data in the first three columns relate to one year later (1976–77) than the information in the other columns which refers to characteristics or operating experiences of the districts for the 1975–76 year.

A few major observations may be made. The number of pupils in the state are declining at all levels. Proportionately, a greater number are minority students and, proportionately, a greater number are being transported. A small increase in professional staff, largely attributable to provision of greater services to handicapped children, in conjunction with the pupil decline, has resulted in declining pupil to professional staff ratios. With the exception of bonded debt per pupil unit, all dollar expenditure, salaries and wealth measures are increasing but at different rates among districts.

Since last year's report, a number of changes have been made in the computation of the statistics used.

First, bonded debt, EARC (property) valuation and income have been related to resident pupils instead of total pupils served. This was felt to be a truer comparison for these districts and more reliable since the figures would not fluctuate with school practices. Since total pupil units include resident pupils and would be the same if there were no nonresident pupils served, the figures for this year would be equal to or greater than those computed in the manner utilized in former years.

Previously, area vocational technical institute (AVTI) staff were included in the professional staffing comparisons. This year, they were removed. By removing these full-time equivalent (F.T.E.) staff, the comparisons between districts relate only to F.T.E. elementary-secondary staff, the pupil-staff ratios relate pupils to

(Continued on page 18)

In order to appreciate the disparities between school districts, the following ranges, averages (means) and percentile rankings of the various indicators are listed.

	Low District	5th Percentile	Average (Mean)	95th Percentile	High District
CHARACTERISTICS					
District Enrollments (Oct. 1976)					
Kindergarten	0	15	138	493	3,942
Elementary Grades 1–6	41	97	811	2,996	21,776
Secondary Grades 7–12	68	131	1,026	3,906	24,841
Total Pupil Units (1975–76)	165	299	2,360	9,038	61,237
Enrollment Trends	81	90	97	107	113
Percent Handicapped	0	0	1.4	2.9	14.1
Percent Non-White	0	0	4.2	7.0	98.5
Percent Attendance	84.3	93.6	94.5	96.5	97.7
Percent Transported	7.5	46.5	67.1	95.5	104.1
Total F.T.E. Staff	15	19	116	425	3,257
Ratio of Pupils to F.T.E. Staff	8.5	11.8	17.4	19.3	21.0
Average Salary F.T.E. Staff	8,124	10,030	13,084	14,234	17,903
Non-Ag Mill Rates	0	39.90	53.99	72.47	117.43
EARC Mill Rates	0	20.99	40.35	51.13	67.12
Federal Sources as a % of Total Receipts	1	2	6	13	37
State Sources as a % of Total Receipts	17	38	55	74	90
EXPENDITURES PER PUPIL UNIT					
Administration	17	29	43	113	186
Instructional Salaries	490	559	711	821	1,098
Other Instruction	38	67	121	146	241
Transportation	16	51	74	140	245
Attendance and Health	0	0	11	13	60
Plant Operation	57	77	115	170	291
Plant Maintenance	3	7	18	41	98
Fixed Charges	24	40	67	94	166
Food Service	18	49	61	92	120
Student Activities	0	0	18	65	117
Transfers	0	4	19	80	173
Community Services	0	0	29	55	308
Capital Outlay	9	29	161	579	2,880
Debt Service	0	0	114	199	275
Abatements	0	0	6	18	99
TOTAL EXPENDITURES	1,085	1,216	1,568	2,050	4,552
State and Local Operating Costs/PU	732	843	1,059	1,256	1,921
Bonded Debt/PU	0	0	1,067	2,013	4,341
1975 EARC Value/PU	51	7,400	15,936	32,648	47,411
1975 Income/PU	1,248	6,489	16,715	20,410	47,577
State and Local Effective Costs/PU	678	809	1,003	1,218	1,893

An Excerpt indicating comparative figures among school districts in Minnesota, UPDATE, Special Report, Summer 1977

Write your state department of education and ask them for this information. You might also want to consider writing the Association of Elementary School Principals for your state or the headquarters for the teachers' association or teachers' union. There is a strong possibility they keep such facts and figures.

The National Center for Education Statistics, an arm of the U.S. Department of Health, Education and Welfare, publishes summaries of the information given out by various state departments of education. Break down the figures to indicate average classroom teachers' salaries and average salaries for other professionals, including curriculum specialists, librarians, remedial specialists, counselors, etc.

In your own school district, the school board minutes may list each and every employee (professional and nonprofessional) and the salary authorized for the year for that individual. Such listing usually will separate regular salary from other pay items for the same person, such as coaching or bus duty. This detailed listing for one year is very cumbersome if your district has more than a hundred teachers. If you want to compare one year to previous years, it is even worse! It may be somewhat better for you to get a copy of the local district's report to the state.

The Problems: Once you've obtained some information on comparative salaries, there are several problems you should be aware of:

1. "Average" salaries alone are virtually meaningless and very unreliable. For example, in New York the school district and the United Federation of Teachers arbitrarily agreed (in 1978) on $19,500 as the "average" salary to help during their negotiations. Even when the average is actually figured out mathematically from the detailed district forms sent to the state, such figures are reliable only at the beginning of the year when the district form is completed. By the time it is published—often a year or so later—any layoffs, retirements, deaths, mid-year hiring, or bonuses, have not been taken into consideration.

   The "average" salary will go up during the year if there are any layoffs, because it is the youngest and lowest paid who are laid off. Retirements and deaths, if they occur in any great numbers, will lower the average salary since these people are probably at the top of the salary range. New hiring during the school year will often lower the average salary of teachers, since those newly hired are often in the lower salary categories. Among administrators, mid-year hiring will sometimes raise the average salary because the school district has hired a more highly paid administrator than the one that was replaced.

2. "Maximum" salary figures alone are not very significant, unless you know how long it takes to get to the maximum. In New York City, it takes half as long to reach the top as it does in Houston, Texas!

3. You must check very carefully to see that the comparisons you have obtained all use the same terminology and include the same professionals. In Minnesota, for example, "Instructional Salaries" includes teachers, principals, consultants, coordinators, librarians, guidance and counseling personnel, psychologists and other instructional resource personnel.

4. Salary figures frequently do not indicate the average number of weeks or months worked. The average salary for twelve-month administrators is probably going to be higher than that for ten-month administrators (all other things being equal—which they seldom are!). Such figures also do not indicate the length of the school day, the number of "teaching" periods per day, or fringe benefits.

5. Some figures are compiled at the *beginning* of the year, either when the budget is adopted or when the actual salaries are authorized. These figures will differ at the end of the school year when actual expenditures are compiled. Be certain you know which figures you are dealing with.

6. "Full Time Equivalent" figures (abbreviated FTE) may be used by your source of information. A staff member spending 100% of his time for the full year is counted as 1 FTE. One employed only half-time as a teacher would be counted as 0.5 FTE. A person employed half-time as a classrom teacher and half-time as the bus coordinator should be counted as 0.5 FTE Classroom Teacher and 0.5 FTE Administrator. Some districts are not too accurate about reporting the actual breakdown.

Other Comparisons with Budgetary Implications

Class size: Apart from the important educational considerations, the budget implications of class size are obvious. Although some make an effort to equate the pupil:teacher ratio with class size, it is in fact usually no real indication of typical class size.

Caution:

1. The "average" class size is usually a meaningless figure. If half the classes in a school district have 40 pupils and the other half have 20, the average is 30. But the pupils are, in fact, never going to be in an "average" classroom. If the special education classes (limited by law in some states to no more than 5-7 pupils to a class) are included in the average, you easily can see that the regular classrooms may run 35 to 38 rather than the 28-30 claimed by the school district on the basis of "averaging"!

2. Teacher:pupil ratio may be listed as 1:18. This is usually derived from the total number of certified teachers compared to the total number of pupils. But how many of those are actually classroom teachers? In many communities counselors, librarians, reading specialists and others are counted as "teachers." In others even principals are counted as "instructional" personnel, and in still others, the ratio given is "Professionals: Pupils," and this is likely to include all administrators as well as all other certified staff persons.

3. Even if the teacher:pupil ratio includes only classroom teachers, you still may not know what the teaching load is, or the number of classes per week, per teacher. You do not know if the teacher:pupil ratio includes teachers who are teaching only one class a day and doing curriculum development work the rest of the time.

4. If you are concerned about how many students are actually in each fourth grade class, for example, and if you can get the actual figures for each class and each teacher, you then may be interested in finding out the absentee rate. For such a study, the "average daily attendance" (ADA), which is often used by the state for reimbursement purposes, is really not relevant. If there are 30 kids

enrolled in your child's fourth grade class, and only 25 show regularly, your child is getting more class attention than he or she would otherwise. But the teacher is still preparing lessons for thirty children, and in classes that make some effort to deal with individual problems, evaluating thirty different children's needs.

Fringe Benefits/Employee Insurance Costs: Comparing the cost of fringe benefits, such as insurance coverage, is sometimes difficult. Although some school districts have a line item in their budget for such insurance, others do not break down such insurance to differentiate among custodians, teachers, administrators or clerks (Illustration 31, pages 127 and 128). Sometimes the costs for all types of insurance are lumped together. You may have to examine the actual invoices (you have a right to!) to determine which costs are clerical fringe benefits, which are teacher benefits, etc. If different insurance carriers are used for different classifications of employees, your comparisons may be somewhat easier.

It is often difficult to determine the costs of new types of insurance coverage in advance. Different parties to the negotiations often make wild guesses as to the costs, but exact amounts often are not known until the list of covered employees actually is submitted and analyzed by the insurance companies. If your district is considering changing carriers or coverage in order to reduce costs, it is a good idea to check with another school district which switched (within the past two years) to see how closely the "actual" figures paid resembled the costs estimated by the agents, the board representatives and the employees' bargaining agent at the time of negotiations. In addition to many really *unknown* factors, there have been questionable practices by insurance agents, or by board members or administrators who deliberately underestimate the cost of changing in order to channel lucrative insurance contracts in a specific direction.

Preparation Time: This item, usually applicable to classroom teachers only, often can increase the quality and the cost of education. A number of school districts—most, in fact—provide duty-free time during the day (apart from lunch periods) to enable teachers to prepare for classes. If

Illustration No. 30
PROFESSIONAL AVERAGE SALARY ETC.

CALCULATOR

Vol. XX, No. 1   Pennsylvania Department of Education   Division of Education Statistics   September 1978

PROFESSIONAL PERSONNEL IN THE PUBLIC SCHOOLS OF PENNSYLVANIA BY SELECTED POSITIONS WITH AVERAGE SALARY, LEVEL OF EDUCATION AND YEARS OF SERVICE, 1977–78

Position	Number	Average Salary	Average Level of Education [1]	Average Years of Service
Total Personnel, Full-Time	130,869	$15,136	5.11	11.92
Administrative and Supervisory				
Executive Director	27	34,659	8.00	28.07
Asst. Executive Director	47	28,616	8.09	24.83
Superintendent, District	500	31,977	8.20	24.56
Asst. Superintendent, District	196	28,217	7.96	22.32
Administrative Assistant	307	24,228	6.49	21.86
Secondary Principal	1,069	24,828	6.77	22.16
Asst. or Vice-Secondary Principal	1,084	22,498	6.64	18.92
Elementary Principal	1,661	23,667	6.70	20.77
Asst. or Vice-Elementary Principal	111	20,697	6.45	17.61
Supervisor	1,198	22,364	6.30	19.19
Classroom Teachers				
Kindergarten	2,527	13,831	4.70	12.16
Elementary	46,479	14,418	4.90	10.91
Secondary	51,126	14,646	5.04	12.07
Combined Elementary-Secondary	2,495	13,324	4.87	10.41
Special Education	7,898	13,601	4.94	7.61
Speech Correctionist	1,213	13,008	4.90	7.17
Head of Department	1,091	19,244	6.17	20.15
Coordinate Services				
Guidance, Elementary	634	16,303	6.18	12.99
Guidance, Secondary	2,568	17,697	6.43	16.51
Guidance, Combined Elementary and Secondary	255	16,324	6.22	15.68
Librarian, Elementary	953	14,122	5.22	11.49
Librarian, Secondary	998	14,922	5.43	13.59
Librarian, Combined Elementary and Secondary	143	14,044	5.22	11.46
Psychologist, District	327	20,916	6.92	13.45
School Nurse	2,077	14,931	4.29	13.01
Specialist	736	15,930	5.87	11.14
Other Positions	3,149	—	—	—

[1] See footnote on reverse side.

Average Salary levels of professional personnel, along with average level of education and years of service. CALCULATOR, Pa. Dept. of Education, September 1978.

Illustration No. 31
EMPLOYEE BENEFITS

800—FIXED CHARGES

	Actual Expenditures 1975-76	Estimated Expenditures 1976-77 June 30, 1977	Budget 1976-77	Proposed Budget 1977-78
Expenses for Fixed Charges				
831—__001 School System Contribution to Employee Retirement (6.65)	589,089	490,000	484,000	520,000
832—__001 School System Contribution to Share of Soc. Sec. Taxes (2.93%) (payroll up to $16,500)	193,015	200,000	200,000	220,000
833—__001 Workmen's Compensation Insurance	24,100	25,000	28,000	37,000
__002 Unemployment Insurance	—	—	—	5,000
833— TOTAL WORKMEN'S COMP & UNEMPLOYMENT INSURANCE	24,100	25,000	28,000	42,000
834— *Employee Insurance, School System Contribution for:*				
__001 Blue Cross & Blue Shield	200,304	325,600	325,300	426,000
__002 Life Insurance	25,000	31,000	46,500	40,000
__003 Major Medical	11,000	15,480	11,900	20,100
__004 Income Protection	20,000	27,000	33,100	35,000
__005 Dental Insurance	12,000	16,100	11,850	33,000
834— TOTAL EMPLOYEE INSURANCE CONTR.	268,304	415,180	428,650	554,100
835—__001 Fire and Extended Coverage Insurance (Burglary, Gen. Liability, Money Security, Employee Blanket Bond and Boiler Insurance)	53,051	48,097	48,100	48,100

(Ill. No. 31—continued on next page)

Excerpt from the Marple-Newton (PA) School District Proposed 1977-78 Budget.

Illustration No. 31
EMPLOYEE BENEFITS

OTHER EMPLOYEE BENEFITS
BLUE CROSS, BLUE SHIELD, and MAJOR MEDICAL H.M.O.—OPTION

During the 1977-80 school years the employer will pay the full premium for each full time professional employee of the school district for Blue Cross, Blue Shield and Major Medical Coverage. Blue Cross will be the 365 day preferred comprehensive plan, Blue Shield will include the prevailing fee 100% coverage, and the Major Medical insurance will provide *$250,000 maximum coverage.* The employer will pay the full premium for family plan insurance coverage for the same Blue Cross, Blue Shield, and Major Medical coverage provided for each professional employee.

Employees and their families may have the option of substituting for the above medical plan, the Health Service Plan of Pennsylvania—a federally qualified health maintenance organization. If this option is taken, the employee will be obligated to pay any difference in cost over the Blue Cross/Blue Shield Plan.

INCOME PROTECTION

The school district will provide a payment of five dollars ($5.00) per month for each full time member of the bargaining unit during the 1977-78, 1978-79, and 1979-80 school year toward the purchase of income protection insurance.

LIFE INSURANCE

A life insurance policy in the amount of one and one-half (1½) times the full-time salary due each member of the bargaining unit to the next highest thousand, with accidental death and dismemberment coverage, will be provided for all full-time employee members of the bargaining unit. Effective date of coverage will be July 1, 1977, July 1, 1978, and July 1, 1979.

DENTAL INSURANCE

The school district will provide 100% prevailing fee basic program Blue Shield dental insurance for all full time employee members of the bargaining unit in the 1977-78, 1978-79, and 1979-80 school years, with the district paying the full premium for individual coverage in all three years.

Excerpt from the Negotiations Agreement Between
Marple Newton School District and Marple Newton Educational Association, 7/1/77.

the work schedule calls for a seven-period day and a teacher is in class for five of those periods, there are obviously additional costs for the substitute or specialist who covers the additional periods. Some districts provide less preparation time for teachers of a single subject, while other districts provide a uniform amount of "prep" time for all. In some areas parents will press for additional prep time if the teachers use written essays on their test. After all, they take a lot longer to grade than multiple choice tests!

Monitoring and other non-teaching duties: If teachers' time is used to supervise lunch hours, bus duty, hall duty and study periods, additional

Illustration No. 31—(Continued)

SUMMARY OF MAJOR BENEFITS (MEDICAL–LIFE)
PROVIDED IN CERTAIN SCHOOL SYSTEMS
— ACTIVE TEACHERS —

CITY	BLUE CROSS					CMS		MAJOR MEDICAL			LIFE INSURANCE		
	S.P. Rm.	Out-patient Rider	SP Mat.	19-24 Rider	Drug Plan	Cent. Plan	Pre/Post Natal	Max.	Deduct.	Co-Ins.	Amt.	AD&D	Cost to Employees
Bridgeport	X	X	X	X	X	X	X	$ 20,000	$ 50	90%	$5,000	X	—
New Haven	X		X	X		X	X	50,000	50	80%	5,000	X	—
Hartford	X					X	X	15,000	50		1.5 of salary		except Dental Plan —50% of family rate
Fairfield	X		X		X	X		30,000	$400 Hosp. $100 Outpat.		50% of salary		—
Greenwich		Blue Cross-Blue Shield						25,000	$100	80%	5,000	X	—for Major Medical —Life Insurance, Dental B.C.—100% less 2.25/mo Individual B.S.—100% less 5.35/mo Family
Stamford		Blue Cross				Travelers					4,000		—
Waterbury	X			*VOL.	X	X	*VOL.	250,000	$100		4,000		—

*Voluntary

Excerpt showing the comparative insurance benefits in selected Connecticut school systems.
From REPORT OF THE TASK FORCE ON TEACHER CONTRACT, Greater Waterbury Chamber of Commerce, 1975.

costs are involved in covering classes which the teachers otherwise could be teaching. Some districts use lower-salaried aides for such duties, while others believe that only teachers can command the respect needed for greater discipline. In comparing costs of your school district to that of others, this is another item to examine.

Salary Advancements/Increments: In most school districts, teachers and administrators qualify for a salary increment for every 4, 8 or ten graduate credits earned—or master's or doctorate degrees. When comparing this benefit in your school district with that of others, be sure to note when the benefit is paid: immediately, or at the beginning of the following year. Note also if the increment is paid for graduate courses which the professionals are *required* to take by the school district or state policy in order to retain their certification. Note also if administrators are being paid such academic salary increments for new certification for positions in which they are already serving—and already collecting the salary of that position.

It also may be interesting for you to compare the nature of the courses for which salary advancement may be given. Does your district compensate for courses that improve teachers' skills only in the fields in which they are presently teaching? Or does it compensate the gym teacher for credits earned in art appreciation? Also, in a district where ten certified counselors (now classroom teachers) are waiting for one of the four counselor positions to open up, does the district continue to compensate teachers for taking graduate credits in counseling? Are teachers paid such increments to take administrative courses? Is the director of social studies paid to take courses in business administration? Many overburdened boards avoid these decisions by establishing a uniform policy.

Miscellaneous Comparisons: Does your school district provide an automobile or car allowance for administrators? Are some allowed to fill up at the district's gas pumps and others not? How does this compare to other districts? Is summer school remuneration tied to the base salary of the personnel hired or is there a flat rate? How much life insurance is provided? What is your district paying for the insurance? How long does it take your teachers to reach the top of the salary schedule? How does this compare to similar school districts?

Chapter 8
Citizen Strategies

I N THE WORDS OF the League of Women Voters: "Most people who take up budget watching aren't, after all, doing it for sport. They want better money management... lower taxes... a new service... better service ... or better citizen access to the budget process."[1]

In this chapter we're going to discuss ways of making your budget study pay off and indicate some of the things parent/citizen groups have been able to accomplish.

Changing Budget Priorities

You may want to work through the budget process for the addition of a new program, a new service, a new position, or even a new duplicating machine for your child's school. Needless to say, the smaller the item or less expensive the service, the more success citizens report in getting it into the budget.

The San Francisco Service Center for Education reports two such citizen success stories: one, the inclusion of a $40,000 bilingual program, and the other an additional $6,000 for a para-professional position.

An Ohio PTA lobbied successfully for a new elementary guidance counselor for the school. Then, they found that parents on the other side of town were blaming them for taking "their" counselor. Apparently the superintendent had "oiled the squeaking wheel" by depriving other youngsters of a needed service. The first group then lobbied for an increase in the cross-town budget!

There is, of course, a moral to this story: when you work for an increase, you must be sure that it is not produced at the expense of needed services. One Pennsylvania group successfully convinced the school board not to close their school, only to find out too late that the money made available was not enough to pay for full-time specialists in art, music, library, counseling and physical education.

Reductions

If you are interested in getting a new program funded or expanded, you may want to search out ways in which existing budget items can be reduced. Such a search also may be undertaken because you are primarily interested in a tax reduction, although you are not likely to achieve that. Probably the most you can hope for is to hold down the tax increases inflation almost dictates.

Do not count on your own school administrators to reveal all possible ways that the budget may be reduced. We have yet to see administrators' salaries reduced or any significant number of lay-offs in maintenance departments, nor do superintendents propose reductions in board members' travel allowances.

Indeed, there are a number of factors which discourage administrators from reducing costs. In schools, as in most bureaucracies, there is no incentive to return unused funds to the treasury at the end of the year, since such an action often serves as grounds for later budget reductions. For this reason, many administrators make it their business to spend their surplus funds on unneeded travel, consultants, equipment or personnel—anything to assure that they will not be cut back next year.

In some communities, administrators act as advisors to the board on teachers' union contract negotiations. Since these administrators' salaries are often tied in some way to the teachers' raise (their raises, for example, may be 1.2% over the teachers'), they may have no interest in sharp negotiating.

In an effort to deal with precisely that kind of problem, and yet give administrators adequate raises, one town in Connecticut provided a fund equal to a percentage of total administrators' compensation from which administrators were paid for outstanding performance based on annual evaluations.

In rare instances, outright criminal activity can add to some school budgets—though such actions are difficult for citizens to detect. In one school district a school board member with over 8 years service was convicted, sentenced to jail and fined $10,000 for illicit dealings in connection with school board contracts. The food service director in a school district near Pittsburgh was convicted, together with the president of a food company, of rigging the bidding process.

Although most school codes require competitive bidding on purchases above a certain minimum, a number of cases have been discovered in which the specifications for the bidding are written by a prospective bidder, acting behind the scenes; moreover, various kinds of services, such as insurance, are often excluded from the bidding process.

In school districts where the operations and maintenance department or the data processing department appear to be overloaded with employees and expenses, it may be worthwhile to investigate the possibility of retaining an outside contractor. Unfortunately, shortsighted, turf-building department managers are often the people asked by the school board to find out what an outside contractor would cost.

In medium and larger school districts where candidates for the school board run active political campaigns, supporters of successful candidates are often given jobs within the school district. Whether citizens can campaign effectively for reductions in such patronage appointments usually depends on how well known this situation is. In some cases, replacement of such school board members may be more productive than working for budget reductions!

One Pennsylvania citizen group finally succeeded—over a three year period—in reducing such political patronage appointments by 25 people. But not because anyone was laid off. It was just a case of attrition—people who resigned or retired or whose terms expired simply were not replaced because the alert citizens worked carefully month by month.

The worksheets we discussed in the last chapter can help you considerably to find costs that are really out of line and to do something about them.

In Antietam Valley School District, irate citizens faced with the possibility of a tax increase of twenty mills organized and successfully pressed to reduce the increase to ten mills by their careful analysis of the budget. The same citizens went on to run a successful write-in campaign to replace three incumbent school directors.

Changing the Budget Process

There is more you can do than just change the budget priorities—which is significant, but often a once-and-done job. You can work to change the process—both external and internal.

Changing the External Budget Process:

Getting a budget process that allows and encourages informed citizen participation often follows a citizen effort to change a particular budget item. In the course of that struggle they become frustrated and angry at the lack of mechanisms that would have allowed them to participate in the budget process before decisions were finalized, and they come to realize that the process needs changes.

"Citizens are entitled to more than an accurate accounting of money in and money out. They are entitled to an understandable explanation of the figures themselves and the reasons behind the choices and decisions,"[2] says a League of Women Voters pamphlet. Although it refers primarily to municipal budgets, suggestions are applicable to school district budgets.

Citizens in Washington, D.C., Massachusetts, Minnesota, Michigan, California and Pennsylvania have reported improvements in the external budget process which originated in response to citizen efforts.

Changing the Internal Budget Process:

What information does your school board require of the administration before making budget decisions? Does the district staff participate effectively in the budget process? These are questions which are of legitimate concern to you if you are interested in efficient and effective management in your school district. Citizen interest in the internal budget process often results from a brief-but-distressing glimpse of the tip of an iceberg.

In one Pennsylvania community, for example, a League of Women Voters observer watched as the school board dutifully passed a $21 million dollar final budget containing reductions of more than $600,000 from the proposed budget presented 30 days before. The only public explanation of that reduction came in the form of an apology from one school board member to the others at the meeting. "I am sorry that you all have not had a chance to see these changes," he said, "but I was working with the assistant superintendent until 5 p.m. today in order to cut out 2 mills on the property tax."

In Minneapolis, citizens made a study of the internal operation of their school district and made the following recommendations:

"The Board of Education should allocate time for themselves as a policy-making governing board to develop a clearer understanding of the Board's role and responsibility in planning and policy formation. Develop the necessary control procedures for the board of education to monitor the activities of the local school and district management.

"Implement a planning, programming, budgeting system that will become fully operative throughout the entire school district during the next two years. Establish formal procedures for implementing existing official policy regarding student and citizen involvement in determining the direction of each local school.

"Establish a district-wide office for comprehensive planning.

"Examine the existing organizational structure in relation to alternative educational approaches.

"Every level of management must develop evaluative criteria and procedures to provide sound data and information from which decisions may be made." [3]

In Massachusetts a citizens' group writes, "We feel that the school committee and administration hardly understand the budget process themselves, and certainly don't concur about the choices to be made prior to the budget formation."

Change Your District Budgeting Process to Zero Based Budgeting?

There is, indeed, a catchiness to the phrase "Zero Based Budgeting" (described on page 55). And there is a political and strategic advantage for a beleaguered school district to adopt or herald their intentions to adopt Zero Based Budgeting. But as a parent/citizen you should be wary, not only of intentional efforts to pull the wool over your eyes, but also of at least two additional problems. The first is that you do not want your school district personnel buried in an avalanche of paperwork—going through the motions, adopting the trappings of ZBB, only to divert attention from real educational needs. If a new budget system is being instituted, you should not hesitate to say, "Show me!" How directly does this new approach relate to improving the educational program and planning? What steps are included to take account of political and personal considerations that enter into every budget allocation process?

A second precaution has to do with the question of motivation—especially motivation of such persons as management consultants, whose professional reputations and, possibly, economic positions will indirectly benefit as the ZBB label gets more widely adopted.

None of which is to say that a change in the school budgeting procedure is not widely needed. Nor that it is not widely resisted by many school officials who prefer doing things the way they've been doing them for the past years. Change of any significant magnitude is difficult to accomplish in any human organization—more so in public agencies where neither profit nor productivity measures act as a motivating factor.

Look carefully at the Multi-Level Standards Based Budgeting concept (described on page 56) and techniques. It admitedly draws from the best features of program budgeting, zero based budgeting, and management by objectives and accomplishes two additional unique tasks. First, it presents for citizens and the board, as well as administrators, the *standards* to be met by the various spending levels (you get what you pay for!). Second, it harnesses the energy that goes into budget preparation by every program/budget manager to the educational program—instead of siphoning off that energy into a strictly administrative, non-educational function. And if you are going to try to change the budget process in your district to the Multi-level Standards Based Budgeting system, consider the technique used in Montgomery County (MD) Public Schools which inaugurated the system on a pilot project the first year before it went system-wide. It is a great deal less threatening that way—and gives the administration time to shake out the bugs present in any new system.

Questioning Resource Distribution

Working to change the budget process—internal and external—along with changing the budget priorities may be less important in your budget study than an effort to work for more equitable distribution of school resources.

You may find that your interest in the budget has been aroused as a result of the recognition that either your kids or some other group of kids are not getting a fair share of the district's resources. You may find that your school district, either through neglect or a deliberate policy of "oil the squeaking wheel," spends a lot more in one school than in another. Sometimes it is obvious. If all new teachers are assigned to one group of schools, parents are bound to realize that they are dealing with both budgetary and administrative discrimination. They are less likely to question these, however, if they are constantly reassured that "everyone" has 35 kids in a class. To find out whether or not that is true, they have to see the board guidelines—which in fact may specify 27 sixth-grade children to each classroom.

The United Bronx Parents organization has been working for a more equitable distribution of resources for a long time. In flyers distributed to citizens, they question (in English and Spanish), "What's wrong with the way the board of education wants to divide up the money?..., If the board would slice up the pie fairly, we could all get together to fight the state and federal governments for a bigger pie. The money must be divided up so that each pupil receives his fair share of the total funds,'"[4] (Illustration 32, page 138).

How You Can Do It

The strategies that you as a citizen choose to utilize in working on your school budget priorities and process will depend on your own style and the receptivity of your particular school district. If you are in a community in which the superintendent and/or the school board want and

Illustration No. 32
PARENT TO PARENT COMMUNICATION

¿QUE ESTA MAL EN LA FORMA QUE LA JUNTA DE EDUCACION QUIERE DIVIDIR LOS FONDOS ESCOLARES?

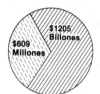

PARA TODOS LOS DISTRITOS LOCALES

$609 Millones

$1205 Billones

PARA LA JUNTA CENTRAL ESCOLAR

LA JUNTA DE EDUCACIÓN SE QUEDA CON MUCHISIMO DINERO

- $1.8 Billon se gastaron el año pasado en educación. Hay 1.1 millon estudiantes en nuestro sistema escolar. Si usted divide todo el dinero entre todos los estudiantes:

$$\frac{\$1,800,000,000 \text{ dinero}}{1,100,000 \text{ estudiantes}} = \$1600 \text{ por estudiante}$$

- Y todavia, muchas de nuestras escuelas estan recibiendo mucho menos de seisciento dollares ($600) por estudiante! *¿Donde está el resto del dinero?*

- La Junta de Educación dice que necesita quinientos millones de dollares ($500,000,000) para poder educar a los estudiantes de escuelas superiores y aquellos estudiantes especiales en educación pero, *sin proveer data, escuela por escuela, que pueda comproba* donde estan los numeritos?

- El setenta y cinco por ciento (75%) de los estudiantes estan en las escuelas elementale a intermedias y todavia la Junta de Educación propone dar a los distritos locales solamente una tercera parte de los fondos.

- Ninguna formula puede ser justa y legal siempre y cuando, la Junta de Educación se queda con la enorme cantidad de dos terceras partes de los fondos bajo su control. Todas esta propuestas "nuevas" formulas serviran solamente para poner a pelear a los distritos unos con los otros.

- SI LA JUNTA DIVIDIERA EL ARROZ CON DULCE EN PARTES JUSTAS Y LEGALES, NOSOTROS PODRIAMOS UNIRNOS PARA PELEAR EL ESTALO Y GOBIERNO FEDERAL POR MAS, MUCHO MAS ARROZ CON DULCE! *LOS FONDOS TIENEN QUE DIVIDIRSE DE UNA MANERA QUE CADA UNO DE LOS ESTUDIANTES RECIBAN UNA PARTE JUSTA DEL TOTAL DE LOS FONDOS ESCOLARES.*

LA JUNTA DE EDUCACIÓN ESTA PROPONIENDO UNA FORMULA PARA CORTAR LOS FONDOS DE AQUELLOS DISTRITOS QUE HAN LOGRADO PODER ENSEÑAR A LOS NIÑOS A LEER.

- La junta propone que los distritos con muchos niños astrasados en la lectura recibiran dinero extra pero, esto quiere decir que tan pronto como dichos distritos empiezen a lograr que los niños puedan leer *perderan los fondos*! Esto es de locos!

- Nosotros no creemos que los niños que hablan español, esto les sea un impedimento o los hagan inhabiles y nosotros no creemos que aquellos distritos que logren enseñar a los niños a leer *bilingualmente*, tengan que perder los fondos por esto. Si acaso se lleva a efecto tal propocision esto es lo que exactamente ha de suceder.

United Bronx Parents flyer, Spanish edition, asking
"What's wrong with the way the Board of Education wants to divide up the school money?"

CITIZEN ADVOCATES FOR READING'S EDUCATION (CARE)

PART II—WORKING PAPER ON READING SCHOOL DISTRICT BUDGET AND FINANCING

A. Believing strongly that taxpayer dollars for education should be used wisely and effectively in accordance with an education plan.

Is the budget of the Reading School District based on . . . . .
1. either short term or long range planning?
2. either general goals or specific objectives?
3. any type of systematic needs assessment and program evaluation?
4. the identification of district-wide priorities by the community? by the board? by the administration? by the faculty? by the students?
5. any equitable guidelines duly adopted by the board (such as pupil-teacher ratio, per pupil expenditures, etc.)
6. any realistic cost/effectiveness analysis of various alternatives?
7. informed, regular community input?
8. thorough personnel evaluations?

B. Believing that citizens have the right to participate in the school budget process and that the community constitutes a valuable resource to assist in the budget decision-making process.

Is the budget process well-coordinated and open to meaningful community participation?
1. Are skilled explanations presented to the community regarding the budget and the budget process? (At regular intervals throughout the year?)
2. Does a single individual take full responsibility for verifying and justifying the total budget?
3. Is there a clear and coordinated organizational structure to encourage informed citizen participation?
4. Does the budget-making process focus consistently on either program costs or on the functional categories (as required by the state accounting system)?
5. Are alternative means of reaching goals studied regularly with anticipated costs and benefits made known?
6. Are salaries fixed by the Board before the adoption of the annual budget?
7. Are comparative intradistrict expenditures made known?
8. Are comparative expenditures and income figures of similar school district made known?

C. Believing that the annual budget is a guide and not a straight jacket, and that the year-round management of budgetary and financial matters is as critical as the budget itself in the effective application of resources.
1. Is the year-round budgetary management fully professional? Well coordinated?
2. Are there systematic internal control procedures readily available for Board and citizens to monitor financial activities?
3. Are policy decisions related to realistic cost figures throughout the year?
4. Are policies related to budgetary and fiscal matters regularly reviewed and updated by the Board?
5. Do the year round practices in budgetary and fiscal matters conform to the school code, Board policies, and prescribed accounting requirements?
6. Is there Board consideration and adoption of specific budgets and public reporting on total expenditures for Funds other than the General Fund (such as the various federal Funds, Bond Revenues, Student and Athletic Activity Funds, Food Service Funds, Museum Funds, etc.?)
7. Is there an effective procedure for long range financial planning in light of the anticipated reduced enrollments and rising costs in the district?

Citizen Advocates for Reading's Education position paper, 1976.

seek citizen participation, you probably will welcome the opportunity to work cooperatively with them. If they emphatically and actively discourage your interest and participation, you may find that you are working in an adversary role. Either way there are a number of general ideas that can be utilized by citizens and citizen groups. These include some of the basic do's and don'ts, getting information, participating in public hearings on the budget, organizing a group and working out general strategies.

Do's and Don'ts—The briefest list

The DO List	The DON'T List
1. Mobilize a group	1. Don't fight other citizens
2. Be persistent	2. Don't give up
3. Start early	3. Don't be distracted
4. Be persistent	4. Don't give up
5. Do your homework	5. Don't be "used"
6. Be persistent	6. Don't give up
7. Follow up	7. Don't be afraid
8. Be persistent	8. Don't give up

You already may know that the oldest (and most successful) technique in the school officials' bag is *DELAY*. They know, and you know also, that most citizens and citizen groups will give up when faced with delay, lack of immediate success, or intimidation. Those few citizens who don't give up usually can be "handled" by co-optation (giving them a job, an appointment or a pacifier of some sort). Other citizens can be distracted by the introduction of an issue like teacher tenure or sex education into a discussion of the budget, or discouraged by repeated assurances that "you've got your facts all wrong, there's nothing to worry about."

Hopefully, you will find yourself working in an atmosphere of cooperation in which your officials will be open and honest with you, receptive rather than manipulative, and anxious to share their problems as well as their successes with you. Whatever your own experience has been in your own community will be the key to the methods you use in making the school budget your business.

Participating in Public Hearings

Sooner or later, if you intend to make the school budget your business, you will be participating in a public hearing. Don't be intimidated. Once you know what the procedure is and what to expect, it is not more difficult than speaking up at any meeting. A public hearing is distinguished from a general information meeting in that a hearing is usually required by state law or school board policy; it usually is designed to give the policy makers—the board—the opportunity to hear what their constituents want. In some communities teachers and union representatives testify as well as students and citizens. A hearing is usually more accurately recorded than a general informational meeting. Minutes are taken and testimony is usually entered into the permanent records of the school board.

Some suggestions you may find helpful:

1 . Call the school district and ask the secretary of the school board for a copy of the minutes of previous public hearings. These will give you an idea of how the meetings were conducted and whether or not the board members or anyone asked questions of those who testified. You may learn if written statements were submitted by all who testified and if the actual testimony was simply a reading of a written statement. You will learn also if the tone of the testimony was formal, informal, emotional, academic, illustrating, etc. It will be helpful for you to note also if any board members or staff persons *answered* any specific questions asked them by persons testifying or in the audience. If so, note if the answers were brief and to the point or simply longwinded. Be aware that sometimes the record is not verbatim.

2. Find out what the ground rules are—early! Do you have to sign up? How much time will be allocated? Must you supply 5 copies of your statement? Most officials *like* to have a written statement, but if it is difficult for you to make copies, let them know it.

3. Find out how the public will be informed about the public hearing. Beware of the "Hardly Anyone Ever Comes To Our Public Hearing" speech. It is often true enough—but how many people are likely to see the official notice of the public hearing if it is buried in tiny print between the *Death Notices* and the *Lost and Found*? You may want to help spread the word, or testify, offering suggestions on how the board can seek broader public participation.

4. Find out what the school district will be doing in advance of the meeting to help citizens identify and recognize some of the impor-

tant issues. No one enjoys going before a public hearing "cold." Few are willing to appear without some good solid information. You may want to help prepare other citizens for the public hearing by sending out an analysis or guide, or by distributing information available from the school district.

5. If you are working with a group, don't hesitate to have as many individuals speak as are willing to make public presentations. Have the spokesperson for your group identify herself/himself as such and have the others identify themselves as simply individual parents or taxpayers interested in the same issue. Be certain, if you are the group spokesperson, to indicate that your statement represents that of the group and that the statement was approved by the majority or unanimous vote of the group's governing council. If, following your presentation as the group's spokesperson, you must speak as an individual, informally, be certain to identify yourself as speaking for yourself.

6. If you don't have an organized group, try to get a number of individuals to the hearing who have similar interest. It may be the basis for organizing a group.

7. Make contacts with other citizens at the public hearings.

8. Make your testimony short and to the point. Summarize your background information and refer to it briefly, indicating that it substantiates or supports your request, and include details with any written testimony you may have—or offer to make it available upon request.

9. End your testimony with one or more specific questions: "When will we know what action you will take on this proposal?" or "Will the board schedule more hearings, public meetings, or citizens' participation opportunities?" Ask the question before your 3 minutes or 15 minutes are up, leaving time for an answer, and remain at the podium or microphone or on your feet until you get one.

10. Follow up the hearings. Write to the board members individually thanking them for their attention (or regretting their absence or preoccupation with other issues). Repeat your concerns. Attend the next several board meetings and other public sessions to see what the board does about the testimony.

Ellen Lurie, an author and longtime activist, points out that typical official responses to hearing testimony include condescending: "You have your facts wrong," or "Oh, we have checked into that and we have that problem under control." She also relates the story of the spontaneous birth of the "People's Board of Education" which took over the platform and conducted its own hearings after the "Board of Miseducation" walked out. She points out the importance of finding out whether the hearings are to be more than merely a "public catharsis." She says, "Nothing makes parents so angry as when they find they have been wasting their time," and, "It is one matter to know that you are powerless; however, it is far more degrading, and dangerous, to have them tell us we have power and then each time we attempt to exercise it, slap us down, overrule us, or invite us to another hearing." She suggests using a public hearing to culminate a campaign, to block a bad decision, to expose the professional staff when it has lied, to make valuable connections, to educate those officials who are still educable, to educate and learn from other citizens, etc. She makes additional suggestions on how to prepare for a public hearing, what to do at a public hearing, and how to force your local school board to hold good public hearings. Her book is a must for anyone involved with the schools.[5]

In *The Citizen and the Budget Process*, The League of Women Voters points out that governmental bodies, including school districts, are increasingly holding budget hearings, and suggests that if this is not the case, citizens should "insist that they be held." In many states they are required by law.

Whether or not budget hearings are anything more than an exercise in futility for citizens depends largely on their timing. If they are not held until a week or less before the scheduled adoption, you can be just about certain there's no time for the board to discuss, consider and intelligently reshuffle the figures in response to any information the hearings provide.

And whether or not you meet with success at a public hearing will depend, most of the time, on what you have done *before* it occurs to lay the groundwork with the administrators, individual board members and other citizens and citizen groups. The League of Women Voters notes in the booklet quoted above, "Sometimes a well done, one-person presentation does the trick. The need is acknowledged, the remedy welcome, the plan put into effect. But not often. If you are speaking just for yourself and your priorities, you are usually competing with other individuals with competing wishes and desires. Often such discord allows officials to keep right on developing a budget in line with *their* priorities negotiated in a community dialogue."

Occasionally you will hit a little bit of luck. You will appear, out of the blue, make a pitch and find that the program is added, the expense reduced, a new procedure adopted—or whatever it is you suggested. You may learn later that there was already a lot of behind-the-scenes pressure from the administrators, or a split board or some new source of available funds, and your testimony served as the catalyst to set the gears working.

But don't expect to be given any credit for bringing about the change. The district's annual progress report will, of course, give the superintendent or the board credit for all new advances—no matter how hard they tried to avoid them initially.

Organizing a Group

There is almost universal agreement on the need for group action to have any impact on the budget process.

Citizens can and do successfully act alone to gather information, analyze budgets, outline process guides and mobilize others. These individual activities are necessary and often will be used by groups interested in effecting changes. But acting alone is time consuming and can be expensive; moreover, the credibility of a citizen acting alone can be questioned and easily dismissed.

The fact is that the more people who are involved in the actual gathering of data, analyzing budgets, putting together position papers and interviewing school officials, the more effective will be the effort to achieve understanding and participation.

Detailed suggestions on organizing citizens' groups are beyond the scope of this book; however, a lot of help is available. We at the National Committee for Citizens in Education have published a primer on organizing entitled *Parents Organizing to Improve Schools*. To find out about this and other useful publications for parents/citizens call our toll-free number 1-800 NET-WORK.

The U.S. Office of Education publishes guides to help Parent Councils organize and recognize their rights; the League of Women Voters at the national level and at many local levels can provide considerable expertise in organizing citizen action. Books and articles by Saul Alinsky are often cited as containing the most effective suggestions for community action. The Parents Union for Public Schools in Philadelphia, the Institute for Responsive Education in Boston, the D.C. Citizens for Better Public Education in Washington, the Minneapolis Citizens Committee on Public Education, the Advocates for Children of New York, and many others throughout the country can give good suggestions for organizing citizens' groups.

If you are a member of an existing organization, work to get it to appoint a specific committee charged with reviewing school budget issues. A good home base for such a committee might be the school PTA, your local branch of American Association of University Women, the Community Action Agency, the local League of Women Voters, or the Chamber of Commerce. Being based within an ongoing and recognized group gives a citizens' budget committee credibility, the use of mailing and printing resources, valuable and experienced membership, and staying power.

On the other hand, a new organization concerned with the school budget can be far more flexible; it will not have to worry about national regulations or about an executive committee with interests in many other issues.

Whichever route you go, remember to seek allies among other existing groups when you are preparing to make presentations to school officials. Sometimes a coalition with a joint operating board is possible. Other times you may want to seek the endorsement of other groups. At still other times you may want to urge such groups to start working on their own on the same issues.

At the Beginning: Any group (whether it is the Budget Review Sub-Committee of Center City PTA, or the Concerned Citizens for Improved Budget Process) should embark on a budget project by asking and answering a number of questions. The newsletter *Apple Pie* (Vol. 3 No. 4) Feb. 1976, published by the Center for the Study of Parent Involvement, presented a list of questions for parent groups to ask themselves that were developed by the Appalachian Child Care Project:

1. Why does our group exist? . . . . Goals
2. What does our group want? . . . . Objectives
3. What can our group do to
   make it happen? . . . . Resources
4. How do we do it? . . . . Strategy
5. Exactly how do we do it? . . . . Task analysis
6. Who will do it? . . . . Assignments
7. When will we do it? . . . . Timeline
8. Are we (Am I) doing it? . . . . Monitoring
9. How do we (I) feel about it? . . . . Self-assessment
10. Did we really do it? . . . . Evaluation
11. So what? . . . . Conclusions
12. Now what? . . . . Recommendations

Getting Group Participants: If you are not starting a school budget study committee as an arm of a larger established membership group you will have to recruit other participants. You may know already that in choosing the name for your organization the word "study" will lose as many potential members as will be gained. Thus a *Budget Action-Study In Our Community (BASIC)* might catch those potential members who are straining at the bit to *"do something about the budget"* as well as those who just want to know what is happening.

Membership/School Employees? Before you begin recruiting membership widely you ought to have a clear statement of purpose and brief by-laws or operating procedures so those coming in will know at once how the organization is to be directed. At the earliest stages it is best if by-laws contain provision for easy amendment. A clause on eligibility for membership and for leadership ought to be included. Citizen groups often are surprised at the willingness, indeed enthusiasm, of the professional educators to participate in citizen groups. Many citizen groups welcome them as resource persons but deny the privilege of holding office or voting to professionals employed by the school district. One citizen group which allowed full participation by school district employees subsequently changed its rule in this respect. The members had noted subtle manipulations by the professionals which almost turned their organization into a puppet show.

The experts have their own agenda, not likely to be identical to that of the lay group. And even if it is, the lay group will have a very hard time developing a sense of ownership about it, and this difficulty alone can undercut any chance of group action. Thus, in addition to dealing with the city and their own incompetence, the lay group must now deal with the experts' agenda.

The experience of most citizen groups indicates that once the group decides on a course of action, endorsement should be sought from other parent and citizen groups, individual teachers and administrators and their associations as appropriate.

In recruiting members, use good public relations techniques to avoid the "Ugh, not another committee" response. If the announcement you send to your local radio station says, "The Budget Action Study In Our Community will meet at 8 p.m. at the YMCA Tuesday evening," it's likely to produce no result. Instead, try, "How much does the school budget allow for your child's reading instruction? Is it enough? Is it too much? Join with others asking these questions Tuesday at 8 p.m. at the YMCA. A meeting for you, the citizen, sponsored by BASIC." Pick an issue of concern to your local community. "How much does the budget provide for administrators' salaries?" "Is next year's school budget going to mean higher taxes?" "Will the new school budget force the closing of your elementary school?"

If your organization has some money you might try placing classified ads in the "personals" or small display ads on the TV pages as the Minneapolis Accountability Project did. Their ad read:

"Help Wanted"

Minneapolis Citizens to join ACCOUNTABILITY PROJECT Task Force evaluating community participation in MPLS Public School planning, operation and evaluation. No req. about age, residence, education or experience. Wed. eve. meetings downtown. For further information please call weekdays, 338-1102.

Some school districts will permit flyers to be sent home with the children announcing forthcoming meetings. In other districts citizens station themselves outside the schools and hand youngsters messages to take home.

General Strategies

The League of Women Voters Education Fund's pamphlet *The Budget Process From the Bureaucrat's Side of the Desk* (1974) is full of helpful hints. It ends with three general suggestions:

"Figure out the Time Table...then you can make your moves at the appropriate times.

"Play by the rules and make them work for you...officials hate schemes that come in half done, inconclusive, not documented, sloppy and not in tune with their procedure.

"Develop credibility. Credibility doesn't mean just whether the sponsors lie or tell the truth—it means whether the sponsors know what they are talking about, whether they can produce...There has to be an expectation of political acceptability. There has to be a feasibility factor...

"In the end, your effectiveness will depend not just on your wanting a worthwhile program or a valid change, but also on your having mastered the rudiments of budget analysis and decided your course of action to take account of the bureaucratic mind—how it works and why." [7]

Quite a different approach is suggested in an article by Gary Wills called "Feminists and Other Useful Fanatics":[8]

"Creative change does not come about by the calm and open discussion of an issue on its merits, leading to a 'verdict' by the judicious public. What happens is quite different: an intransigent minority makes a nuisance of itself until most of the public says, "All right, give them what they want, shut them up."

Wills, of course, is talking about national moral and political issues including suffrage, civil rights, prohibition—not school budgets. But reports from citizens working to change their school budget or the budget process in communities in almost every state agree with his assessment: "Politicians do not bring about change. Their effort, very useful in its way, is to prevent change—to slow it down, blunt it, absorb it. That's why they need such persistent prodding before they respond at all...."

A Taxpayer's Guide to School Finance was published by the Palo Alto Unified School District in February 1973. This 16-page handbook, which was designed to explain the budget-making process in general terms, contains a section called, "How you can have a voice in what's decided," which included the following:

1. Become informed in a general way about the entire budget-making process, and the constraints which affect the outcome. If your opinions are to be useful to the board, you must make suggestions within the realm of what's possible.

2. Decide what your priorities are, and why you feel as you do.

3. Outline your views in a letter to the board.

4. Speak up at one of the public meetings when the board will be discussing the budget. The dates of these meetings are April 3, June 5, June 19, and August 10.

5. Join the efforts of one of the organizations that is active in the budget process. Each year a number of organizations express their views about the Operating Budget. Among these are the League of Women Voters, the Forum for Education, school PTA units, and the Palo Alto PTS Council.

   It should be pointed out the state legislature, the state department of education and even the U.S. Congress have a great deal to say about the way the school district may spend its money and the amount of money it will have to spend. You can have an influence on the local budget-making process by expressing your views on school finance to state legislators and U.S. Congressmen.[9]

The San Francisco Service Center for Public Education suggests "strategies and tactics everyone can use" to get a new program budgeted.

"To best work for a new program, first organize yourselves:

1. Assign members of your group to cover all board meetings.

2. Assign individuals to attend all board committee meetings.

3. Have the same individual contact the same board member by letter and phone repeatedly; decision makers will remember individuals as well as groups.

4. Find out who in your community can write a good proposal for the program you want.

"The following are specific lobbying techniques:

1. Bring a group to public meetings. Most impressive is a united group of parents, children, teachers and principals together.

2. Meet with the district staff before going to the board. Know in advance the staff recommendation on your program.

3. Collect background information yourselves. This may mean finding out if there's a real need for your program, what individual principals think of it, or how much it will cost. Facts, statistics, and pupil cost demonstrate that you've done your homework!

4. Write factual, business-like letters and demand a written response...if at all possible, visit the decision makers in person.

5. Get letters of support from other city organizations and from state and local politicians. Refer to these endorsements in public meetings.

6. Contact all board members before a meeting so you can predict the votes. Have alternatives ready if the votes look discouraging.

7. Find out when and where you must sign up to speak before a public board meeting or at a public hearing. Send or hand in a written request to speak before the deadline. Check with the board secretary to find out where you appear on the schedule.

8. Bring a tape recorder to all public meetings and to interviews.

"Some specifics:

1. Find out who in the administration is responsible for the budget and plan to meet him/her in person or contact them by letter.

2. If you have difficulty trying to reach someone by phone to set an appointment in advance, go to the central administration building in person to meet him/her. Once there, remain in an office until someone agrees to meet with you.

3. Always bring at least two other people in order to be sure of the outcome of any meeting.

4. If no action results from your meeting, arrange to speak with the next highest administrator.

5. Invite board members to sit in on these meetings.

6. Be thoroughly prepared with information, strategies for presenting it, and alternative plans for the program.

"Above all, remember to:

1. Have your own group organized so everyone knows *what* is happening *when* and you can avoid duplicating each other's work.

2. Be informed about the costs, problems and solutions of your program.

3. Contact people individually and in advance of meetings.

4. Persist." [10]

We would add to this list, begin by picking an issue you have a good chance of winning, at least initially. Take on one issue at a time and see it through—don't use the shopping list approach. And finally, remember that the school board plays a major role in determining school budgets. So you should think seriously of having your group run a candidate for school board membership.

FOOTNOTES
(Chapter 8)

[1] League of Women Voters Education Fund, THE BUDGET PROCESS FROM THE BUREAUCRAT'S SIDE OF THE DESK, 1974.

[2] League of Women Voters Education Fund, THE CITIZEN AND THE BUDGET PROCESS: OPENING UP THE SYSTEM. Washington, 1974.

[3] Minneapolis Citizens Committee on Public Education, THE MANAGEMENT OF EDUCATIONAL RESOURCES: A STUDY OF THE MANAGEMENT AND DECISION-MAKING PROCESS OF THE MINNEAPOLIS PUBLIC SCHOOLS, 1973.

[4] United Bronx Parents. Undated flyer to parents.

[5] HOW TO CHANGE THE SCHOOLS: A PARENT ACTION HANDBOOK ON HOW TO FIGHT THE SYSTEM. Random House, a Vintage Book, 1970.

[6] League of Women Voters Education Fund, THE CITIZEN AND THE BUDGET PROCESS: OPENING UP THE SYSTEM. Washington, 1974.

[7] League of Women Voters Education Fund, THE BUDGET PROCESS FROM THE BUREAUCRAT'S SIDE OF THE DESK. Washington, D.C. 1974.

[8] Wills, Gary "Feminists and Other Useful Fanatics." HARPERS MAGAZINE, June 1976.

[9] Palo Alto Unified School District, A TAXPAYER'S GUIDE TO SCHOOL FINANCE. Palo Alto, California, 1973.

[10] The San Francisco Service Center for Public Education. ACCESS TO THE SCHOOLS: A GUIDE TO THE SAN FRANCISCO SCHOOL BUDGET, 1974.

Chapter 9

Preparing a Guide for your Community

PREPARING a guide for your own community is a demanding but rewarding undertaking for any citizen or citizen group. If you already have successfully figured out your district's budget process, getting it all down on paper and into print will present you with mainly technical decisions. On the other hand, if you are about to undertake an in-depth study of the budget process, which could take several months, there are a number of things you may want to do immediately. Any one of these short-term efforts, depending on your interest and the issues in your community, will provide good material for the guide and also may arouse other citizens' interest and get them to work with you on preparing it.

Short-term Efforts

1. Distribute widely (or insist that the school district distribute widely) all the information on the school budget that the district already has prepared. This may mean only the budget calendar; it may mean last year's budget; it may mean an announcement of a public hearing; it may mean a popularized budget; and, if you are lucky, it may mean a neat little handbook that the district itself has prepared to aid citizens in understanding the budget process.

2. Prepare your own simple announcements of the budget calendar and forthcoming public hearings, urging citizens to participate. Distribute these to parents, to the media, to organizations.

3. Prepare and distribute questions relating to the budget or budget process. The questions can be provocative, designed to arouse

citizen interest, or they can be neutral, that is, seeking objective information. Or they can reflect some of your impressions about the budget process, impressions that haven't been checked out enough to make you comfortable with recommendations (Illustration 32, page 138).

4. Prepare and distribute an analysis of your district's school budget for this year. It can be in narrative form, or in simple chart form derived from the worksheets we discussed earlier in this book. Clearly this involves considerable effort. But at least you may not have to depend on interviews to get it prepared. Later this can be included as part of a more general guide to the budget process.

5. Modify the figures set by school officials to some which you would prefer to see. If the timing of your effort coincides with the release of the proposed budget for the forthcoming year, it is bound to arouse some interest in the budget. District officials and other citizens are likely either to disagree or defend such specific modifications (Illustration 33, page 156).

6. Any other projects you and/or your group might decide to carry out as a short-term effort undoubtedly will be useful in the longer-term effort to prepare a guide.

Why Prepare a Guide for Your Own Community?

Action Research: At the beginning of this handbook, a number of general reasons why the school budget is your business were cited. In your own community you will recognize additional reasons to want to get other citizens involved in understanding and participating in the school budget process. Even so, a number of citizens still will be reluctant to undertake a project like the preparation of a guide, which is time consuming, difficult and often quickly outdated. Obviously, *your* priorities and values will determine whether you spend time preparing a guide to your school budget process or some other school-related activity.

A Citizen's Job? You also may conclude that you do not want to do the job you are paying school administrators to do. This reaction is understandable; but, you should know that when school officials prepare a guide, it will be their priorities that receive emphasis. Even the district-prepared guide usually cited as "the best" by citizen groups *and* fellow professionals comes in for criticism by some citizens within the community.

The case for preparing a guide for your own community is found in The Institute for Responsive Education's *Action-Research* publication.

"It is not so much that action-research leads to action, though that is certainly true. Action research *is* a form of action. It provides a means of organizing large numbers of people around well-defined, short-term jobs. It engages people face to face with the problem. It builds a base of mass support for a given problem—and in doing so translates research into politics for politically reticent people. It is a way of thinking clearly, getting the facts, and acting collectively on almost any problem.

"An action-research program is one in which numbers of people can be organized to define problems and gather facts so that research becomes a form of empowerment and action. Action-research is a form of collective citizen power.... Action-research can help weed through the tangles of urban affairs. It can develop competence within a lay group, and it can permit that group to take advantage of expertise without being smothered by the experts agenda...."

How To Do It—Some Suggestions

Reminder: Keep a permanent notebook. Write everything down. Once you have decided to prepare a guide in general terms on the format, will it be just a step-by-step report on what the process is supposed to be? Are you going to point out what it is in reality? Are you going to make recommendations for changing or improving the process? Are you going to help citizens understand the internal and the external budget process? Be flexible, but start out with an idea of where you are going.

Consulting With School Officials: Decide in advance at what points you are going to consult with the school administration. As we suggested earlier, it would be wise to gather and review all available printed information before arranging interviews with school officials. Once you have

Illustration No. 33
PROPOSED BUDGET ALTERNATIVES

Col 1	Col 2	Col 3	Col 4	Col 5	Col 6
Code	Changes indicated in this column are changes (up or down) in current year's figures unless otherwise indicated	Figures in these columns taken from School District's budget of 5/28/75		Figures in these columns are being submitted as a citizen's alternative	
0200	Instruction	Estimated Expenditures 1974–75	Proposed Budget 1975–76	Citizen's Proposed Budget 1975–76	Savings or additions 1975–76 budget
0211	Salaries, Principals & Assistants . . . . Add to 1974–75 figures 5% salary inc. ($24,250)	$485,000.00	$514,600.00	$509,250.00	− $5350 saving
0212	Salaries, Supervisors	$328,000.00	$374,850.00	$344,400.00	− $30,450 saving
0213	Salaries, Teachers . . . . Add to 1974–75 figures 10% salary increase ($844,719)	$8,447,190.00	$9,448,280.00	$9,291,909.00	− $156,371 saving
	Add to 1974–75 figures for substitutes ($50,000)			$50,000.00	+ $50,000 added
0214	Salaries, Librarians . . . . Add to 1974–75 figures 10% salary raise ($20,200)	$202,000.00	$246,000.00	$222,200.00	− $23,800 saved
0216	Salaries, Other Inst Staff . . . . . Add to 1974–75 figures 10% salary raise	$100,000.00	$92,250.00	$110,000.00	+ $17,750 added
0219	Salaries, Clerks & Lunch Aides . . . . Add to 74–75 figures 10% raise ($46,047)	$460,475.00	$479,548.00	$506,522.00	+ $26,974 added
0218	Salaries, Matrons (add 10% to 74–75)	$47,000.00	$57,000.00	$51,700.00	− $5300 saving
0221	Textbooks . . . . Deduct from 75–76 proposed for book covers ($5000.00)	$148,114.00	$116,034.00	$111,034.00	− $5,000
0222	Teaching supplies	$347,604.00	$357,732.00	$357,732.00	− − −
0223	Library books and supplies . . .	$41,530.00	$34,443.00	$34,443.00	− − −
0224	Audio Visual Materials . . . . Deduct from 75–76 budget $42,218.00 for materials Use materials from Instructional Media Services approx ($30,000–$20,000)	$29,390.00	$42,218.00	$30,000.00	− $12,218
0229	Other materials & supplies . . .	$13,507.00	$20,301.00	$20,301.00	− − −
0231	Expenses, Inservice Training .	$3,500.00	$7,000.00	$7,000.00	− − −
0239	Other Expenses of Instruction	$34,871.00	$61,663.00	$43,663.00	− $18,000 saving
	This appears to include the following items according to the various committee budgets presented to the public on 5/21/75, although the several totals on the committee budgets for this category (0239) exceed the amount listed in the 5/28 proposed budget:				

A citizen's proposals for budget alternatives. Excerpts from 10 page document.

completed the review of the literature, you will have to meet with some school officials. Do you want to start at the bottom and work up? That is, interviewing individual principals and teachers first to find out what their role in the budget process is? Or, do you want to go to the superintendent, first, and find out his recommendations on whom to see? After the interviewing stage has been completed and you have gathered information, are you going to check it out? Are you going to find out directly from the department heads, or the high school principal, or the director of library services what their role has been?

Additional questions may include: Are you going to find out if the superintendent's description of the budget process related only to the "Administration" and "Instruction" portion of the budgets, while the "Maintenance" and "Operation" portions are formulated outside the realm of the usual budget process? What will you do if two sources tell you that, "All the teachers participate in establishing budget priorities," while a third says, "Not in our school! The principal sent in those requests on her own!" Do you wish to allow the administrators to check out the accuracy of your perceptions? Will you allow them to review your whole budget guide before you go to press? If you are working with a group, it is best to clarify some of these alternative approaches at the beginning.

Reviewing Previous Budget Process: Review the actual budget process of the previous year. Even if you are told that the whole process has changed this year, a review of the previous year's process may help give you some perspective. It also will allow you to judge whether the new process is an improvement or a step backwards. Review the news accounts, if any, of the public hearings, the adoption of the budget and any other news items relating to the school budget. Then ask the school's public information officer to let you look through the file of all material sent out to parents last year. Make notes on the dates and manner of announcing budget matters, opportunities to discuss needs assessments, and other related matters. Ask to look over the various internal memos that laid out specific budget responsibilities last year. Look over the results of the needs assessment surveys. Review the minutes of the elementary principal's meetings with the budget officer, and the minutes of the Property and Maintenance Committee of the board. If you have the time, energy and cooperation of the school administration, you may find this review most enlightening. Seldom, if ever, does an institution like a school district change overnight. Even a new superintendent finds it difficult, if not impossible, to sweep out all the procedures in only a few months. So expect to make your own judgment about what is theory and what is reality in your school district's budget process.

Gaining Perspective: Gain as many different perspectives as possible when learning about the budget process. After you have reviewed thoroughly the printed material, the superintendent or budget officer should be interviewed for an overview. Interview the individual principals in different parts of town. Interview the teachers' union leader. Interview a few of the teachers in various schools. Interview the supervisors, department heads and assistant superintendents.

Ask each of these people specifically to describe their role in the school budget process—this year and last year. Then ask each about his or her perception of how the budget process works. Reassure them that you are interested in their perception rather than the "official" line. Take another person or a tape recorder and keep accurate notes.

Recommending Changes: A number of local guides to the school budget process include recommendations for improving the quality or quantity of citizen participation. Other recommendations relate the manner of establishing priorities, needs assessments and presentation of the budget. During the interviews with school officials at all levels, it is a good idea to set aside an "off the record" time to solicit the officials' suggestions on improving the budget process. All such "off the record" suggestions should be considered—without attribution—by your committee to determine which you may want to include as recommendations to the district. Anonymity is usually necessary to avoid jeopardizing the jobs or reputations of cooperative officials whose suggestions may be implicitly or explicitly critical of their superiors or board. Your committee must be prepared to substantiate and support any recommendations which you ultimately decide to include in a guide to local budget process.

Charting the Process: A chart of the budget process can be helpful. If your school district does not have one, make it up yourself, based on the

Illustration No. 34
HANDBOOKS FOR BUDGET ANALYSIS

WYOMING TAXPAYERS ASSOCIATION
HANDBOOK FOR BUDGET ANALYSIS

Section I

Introduction:

Every couple of years the people go to the ballot box and elect federal, state, and local officials. All too often, however, this summarizes the total involvement of the typical citizen in the affairs of government. Good government does not come that easily. If left to their own devices public officials have only their own judgment, and the pressure of organized interest groups on which to make decisions. This handbook is designed to help you improve your control over the affairs of local government, and extend them beyond the ballot box.

Of course, in order to move you to do something about local government spending you have to be interested in the idea. Here is an example which may set your brain whirring, and your feet moving: (If the example seems too high or too low you can figure your own situation by following the example and supplying your own income and property values).

A. This hypothetical taxpayer-voter owns a home and lot valued at $30,000 replacement cost. His assessed valuation is 20% of the replacement figure, or $6,000. Last year the two governmental units discussed in this handbook had the following typical mill levies.

County		School District	
12.0	— operating levy	23.0	— operating levy
1.1	— bonds & interest	12.0	— countywide school tax
		5.29	— state school levy
13.1	— Mills Total	4.75	— bonds & interest
		45.04	— Mills Total

13.1 mills + 45.04 mills = 58.14 mills = .05814 × $6,000 for a property tax bill of $348.84.

B. His income was $10,000 gross. After federal taxes he had about $8,500 for personal consumption. $1,800 went for mortgage payments and $850 went for savings and other non-taxable expenditures. Everything else went for family expenses. $12 of the total gasoline taxes he paid were returned to the county; $30 of the sales taxes he paid returned to the county; and there's the undetermined amount he paid to the state in these taxes that came back to his school district.

(Ill. No. 34—continued on next page)

Excerpt from citizen handbook printed by the Wyoming Taxpayers Association.

information you gather from your interviews and printed material (Illustration 24, page 81).

Putting It All Together: Be certain to leave yourself plenty of time to go back and check out facts and figures, if necessary. If your committee is to review the final draft the night before it is to be run off, be prepared for some conflicting perceptions. "Oh, no. That isn't the way I heard it!" If you have taped the interviews, checking it out may be easy. If you have circulated among all committee members the essence of each interview or a summary of each document *as you went along*, there will be fewer misconceptions at the final stages.

Illustration 34—(*Continued*)

process. The District's proposed timetable for developing the 1974-75 budget is reproduced on page 15.

This budget request form shows how much each program received for the current school year for teacher salaries, supplies, equipment, maintenance, etc. It serves as the basis for estimating the entire budget for the upcoming school year. The most flexible areas in the budget are supplies and equipment. Teacher and administrator salaries are the most inflexible since these amounts are locked into the number and kind of personnel necessary to run programs. If, in filling out a budget request form, an administrator seeks additional program money, he must justify that additional request in writing. In proposing an entire program, he must also set forth the objectives that program will meet.

At the school site level, principals serve as "program managers." They consult with their staffs to form the school's total budget request. The heads of the district-wide programs operating independently of school sites also act as "program managers." Both principals and these program heads fill out the yearly budget request forms mentioned above. They submit these forms to the Office of Budget Planning by the first week in January. There the requests from all over the District are analyzed, coded, and typed into a computer. The computer compiles all individual budget requests into the original form of the annual district-wide budget.

What is the Budget Decision-Making Process?

The next step in the budget process is a review of all requests by certain administrators acting as "budget managers." These are individuals who are formally held accountable for a specific program in the budget. The following administrators will serve as budget managers in developing the 1974-75 school budget: Associate Superintendents Reiterman (Administration of Services) and DeLara (Operations and Instruction) and Assistant Superintendents Pivnick (Elementary Schools); Boisson (Junior High Schools); Kauer (Senior High Schools); Dean (Special Education); Cobb (Community Relations); DelPortillo (Bilingual Education); Mahon (Special Programs); Minkler (Compensatory Education); Silverstein (Planning). During the third week in January, these budget managers review program requests. They decide which money remains in the budget and which cuts are necessary.

Once the budget managers have finished their review and made modifications, a report is prepared to justify any changes made. That report is circulated down to the program managers who

Excerpts from ACCESS TO THE SCHOOLS: A GUIDE TO THE SAN FRANCISCO SCHOOL BUDGET, a 39 Page booklet published by the Service Center for Public Education.

It's a good idea to use a binder for the report that makes it possible to add or remove pages, so that it can be kept up to date.

Use position titles in the text (and on the chart) instead of specific names. Then, list on a separate sheet the titles, names, and telephone extensions of all whose positions are mentioned in the text. In this way, you will be able to update the guide easily.

Include the names of the committee preparing the guide. List at least one organizational telephone number and address (of the budget chair-

Illustration 34—(Continued)

originally made the requests. The justifications of budget cuts are also circulated upward to the Division Heads, the Superintendent, and the Board of Education. This modified budget goes back to the Office of Budget and Planning. There the reworked budget is punched into the computer. It prints out a new program budget. This one reflects all changes made by the budget managers.

The second level of the budget review process consists of Division Heads. They are: Associate Superintendents Reiterman and DeLara and Assistant Superintendents Pivnick, Boisson, Kauer, Dean, Kennedy, and Cobb. Again, these individuals have a new opportunity to propose changes in the budget as it has evolved to date.

The third level of the review process starts after changes made by the Division Heads have been added to the program budget. Near the end of March, the Superintendent's Cabinet meets to study the budget. Here most final administrative decisions and changes are made. This year the Cabinet members are: DeLara, Reiterman, Boisson, Pivnick, Kauer, Kennedy, Cobb, Dean, Wire (Public Information), Cannarozi (Labor Relations), Porter (Fiscal Office), and the District's Legal Advisor (currently vacant).

By the time the Cabinet sits down to review the budget in late March, the district has some pretty firm estimates of how much money it can expect to take in for the following school year. The twelve ranking administrators who make up the Cabinet know what the real operational needs of the District are likely to be for the coming year. Thus it is the Cabinet which sets the operational priorities for spending extra dollars or cutting back programs to free money for under-funded but critically-needed activities. For example, next year the District will have to allocate money to cover the extra costs of busing children during building reconstruction. If the budget is tight—in other words, if the budget requests are equal to the estimated District income—the District will have to take out money from some programs to provide additional transportation money.

The Cabinet is the arena in which major decision-makers can make trade-offs between the various operational units and divisions of the school district. It is the last opportunity for administrators to influence the budget before it is finally sent to Superintendent Morena's office. In most cases, the Superintendent will approve the Cabinet's recommended budget after some minor revisions of his own. Since most Cabinet members are familiar with the

(Ill. No. 34—continued on next page)

man, the president, or the secretary) so that other citizens can contact you directly if they want to offer suggestions for your next project!

What Other Citizen Groups Have Done

The Wyoming Taxpayers Association, the San Francisco Service Center and the D.C. Citizens for Better Public Education have developed handbooks to help their members and other citizens (see Illustration 34, pages 159 through 167).

Illustration 34—(*Continued*)

In 1971, the new Superintendent of the District of Columbia Public Schools, Dr. Hugh Scott, observed,

The image of the Public Schools of the District of Columbia is poor. This negative image has been created by the continuing downward trend in reading and other academic skills, the high dropout rate and the presence of crime, violence and drugs in the schools.

No further study is needed to prove that the public schools of the District of Columbia are not doing as well as they should. And yet no remedies have been developed for the basic defects most evident—and painful—to students, parents, and taxpayers: outdated and inefficient methods of instruction and teacher trainings, irrelevant curriculum, inadequate and inappropriate books and materials.

These defects are the result of a deeper, more pervasive problem which must be explored: the inability of the D.C. school system to respond to the need for change and improvement, to give our children the educational services they require. The two basic wings of the school system, the administrative and the instructional, behave as though they do not communicate with, or, care about, each other.

Bureaucratic Confusion

The average citizen—and even the Board of Education member—who tries to learn how administrative and instructional decisions are made, is confronted with a puzzle almost impossible to resolve.

- Divided and constantly changing authority makes responsibility for decisions impossible to locate.
- Policy decisions get lost in the bureaucratic maze of paperwork, obfuscating procedures, and constant buck-passing.
- Decisions made by teachers about curriculum and teaching materials are undercut by administrative decisions higher up.
- Deliveries of materials and services to the school and classroom are erratic or non-existent.
- Administrative aides in the central office, performing general clerical duties, are more highly paid than the teachers who have direct contact with children.

Excerpt from FINANCING THE D.C. PUBLIC SCHOOLS,
A Budgeting and Planning Guide for the Citizen.

Illustration 34—(Continued)

• Adequate performance in a given job is not defined; promotion and tenure of personnel in specific jobs are based on factors other than job performance.

Inadequate Records

The citizen who begins to explore the financing and operation of the D.C. schools is soon confronted with a depressing fact: the school administration does not seem interested in keeping the kinds of records that are essential for any well-run enterprise. Some statistics—school-by-school reading scores, for example—have had to be forced from the administration by repeated Board of Education demands. Indices such as the number of children on the waiting list for Special Education are deceptive, for no effort is made to inform parents of all services available nor to identify all children needing such services. (The fact that tuition grants can be obtained for private schooling for handicapped children is a well-kept secret from most poor parents.) Other figures given out by the schools, including school-by-school and city-wide per pupil expenditures, are conflicting and unreliably calculated.

This lack of adequate record-keeping is not due to insufficient means. In 1969, the school system installed a computer data processing capability which could produce any desired information printouts, if the basic data were supplied and the proper buttons pushed. Unfortunately, the ability and determination to use this capability to produce all needed information seems absent.

Such unprofessional disinterest in thorough data-keeping was emphasized in a recent court decision in the long-running *Hobson v. Hansen* case. At one point during months of complex legal maneuvers, the school administration was asked for an analysis of scores on reading tests of children bused to less crowded schools, to show if reading scores had improved. Judge J. Skelly Wright said of the school administration, the defendants:

On February 16, 1971, however, defendants moved the court to rescind this order on grounds that it "imposes an unduly burdensome task upon the proper defendants and that the order will not lead to probative evidence" The gist of the memorandum in support of defendants' motion was that no systematic records of test results had been kept, and that those bused children who had been tested had been given different brands of tests for which conversion scales are unavailable—thus rendering meaningful comparisons impossible. While the court does not charge defendants with a

(Ill. No. 34—continued on next page)

Illustration 34—(Continued)

TABLE 2

COMPARISON OF OPERATING EXPENDITURES PER PUPIL, PROFESSIONAL STAFF PER 1000 PUPILS, AND TEACHER SALARY RANGES FOR SELECTED LARGE CITIES AND WASHINGTON, D.C. SUBURBAN SYSTEMS, FY 1969

School System	Operating Expenditures Per Pupil (all funds)[b]	Professional Staff Per 1000 Pupils[a]	Teacher Salary Range[c]	
			Beginning	Maximum
New York, N.Y.	1,031	54.5	6,750	13,900
Cty, Va.	1,008	45.6	6,400	16,000
N.Y.	960	52.5	6,800	12,510
Philadelphia, Pa.	941	N.A.	6,700	13,300
Washington, D.C.	839	58.1[e]	7,000	13,440[e]
on Cty, Va.	N.A.[d]	55.6	6,200	13,702
Montgomery Cty, Md.	801	50.8	6,340	13,377
San Diego, Cal.	801	N.A.	6,650	14,010
Seattle, Wash.	801	48.3	6,175	12,250
Prince George's Cty, Md.	747	51.0	6,200	13,640
Baltimore, Md.	707	49.3	6,500	12,400
Cleveland, Ohio	682	N.A.	6,250	11,000
Boston, Mass.	680	55.2	6,500	12,350

From D.C. Public Schools, *Proposed Operating Budget for FY 1971*, August XX-6.
From D.C. Public Schools, *Proposed Operating Budget for FY 1971*, August XX-9.
From National Education Association, *Salary Schedules for Teachers*, Research Report 1966-R-3 1966, pp. 26-107.
1968 figure not available; was $810 in '67-'68.
Cited figure from D.C. Public Schools, *Proposed Operating Budget for FY 1969*, p. 23-XX-2.
Report prepared by the District government in June 1970, professional staff per 1,000 shown as 63.0 for FY 1969 (Government of the District of Columbia).
    Materials Federal Payment (p. 1-4). We have no way to tell which is the figure: this is only one of many instances in which we have found conflicting figures.

Needs

In spite of relatively high expenditures, many students are not getting the education they need. For example, the board of Education has committed itself to provide early childhood education to all children, yet it is currently serving fewer than 2,000 out of an estimated population of 20,000 four and

Excerpt from FINANCING THE D.C. PUBLIC SCHOOLS, A Budgeting and Planning Guide for the Citizen, published by the D.C. Citizens for Better Education.

Illustration 34—*(Continued)*

five year olds. And many of the handicapped children in the District are not enrolled by the schools at all. The 5-year plan issued by the Department of Special Education in June 1969, indicated that the school system was directly serving only 40% of the estimated number of handicapped children in the city.[10] (Many educators are convinced that the incidence of handicapped children in urban areas is significantly higher than the nationwide estimate of 6 to 10% of the school-age population on which the District's estimate is based.) Also, those classes in operation in the District are almost exclusively for younger children; little provision is made for handicapped teenagers and young adults.

In the whole area of career-vocational training, the school system's goal is to provide all secondary students, college-bound as well as others, with employment skills and opportunities to discover their career interests. In '69-'70, senior high school enrollment was almost 19,000: vocational programs served less than 3,000.[11]

Summary of Per Pupil Expenditure Problems

It is possible, and even probable, that some of the District's current resources are being spent inefficiently. A thorough management study of the school system is essential to identify weaknesses. (See Part V. p. 55.) Nevertheless, cost comparisons with other large urban systems indicate that Washington's relatively high per pupil expenditure figure is deceptive. When unusually high expenses for state plus city services, professional staff, maintenance cost, and fixed charges are taken into account, the District is actually receiving relatively less funds to handle its severe educational problems than most similar urban systems. The figure is even more deceptive when used in comparison with suburban school systems where wages, services, and land are cheaper and the educational problems less severe. To justify the school system's requests for funds, administrators must produce a fully-documented per pupil figure which realistically compares to figures for other school systems.

SCHOOL CONSTRUCTION

In Part V on page 51, we discuss some limitations on funds borrowed from the U.S. Treasury, and how this affects the construction of D.C. schools. Other factors peculiar to the District of Columbia contribute to long and costly construction delays.

Congressional Review

The city is required to submit construction plans, down to

(Ill. No. 34—continued on next page)

Illustration 34—(Continued)

Citizen Participation

We suggest that community committees be established for the school to consult with the school staff and to review the summary of the Superintendent's proposed budget. These citizens would be elected by the community, perhaps through the school's parent organization, rather than being appointed by the Board of Education member representing that ward. (The most important reason for election rather than appointment by Board members is the need for wider contact with the community. Board members would naturally appoint citizens with whom they are already in communication; an election would give new voices a chance to be heard.) At senior and vocational high schools, students selected by the student government should participate on the committee.

The primary function of the community committee should be to review the summary of the Superintendent's proposed budget patterns of the specific conditions, resources, and needs of their school. They should compare his high priority programs with other possible programs, taking note of the estimated costs of each. Needs may be identified for which programs have not been proposed; the committee might suggest priorities for the development of programs to meet those needs.

This plan would allow the community committees to serve a vital function so necessary in a large city school system, providing the community's response to school administration programs. With the benefit of this counsel, the Superintendent can amend the proposed budget to give the Board of Education a document more accurately reflecting administration and community priorities.

Resolved Problems

For FY 1972, the school administration prepared a document called "Highlights" of the proposed budget. The "Highlights" included a brief discussion of goals and budget requests. The document illustrates some of the major inadequacies of the budget process. In expectation of inadequate funds to meet the required costs of current staffing and programs, the document named certain areas areas where cuts could be made by so-called "collection of funds."

One recommendation was a 25% cut in contractual services, with no indication of what those services are, other than the general phrase "use of consultants and contracts mainly in

Excerpt from FINANCING THE D.C. PUBLIC SCHOOLS, *A Budgeting and Planning Guide for the Citizen, published by the D.C. Citizens for Better Education.*

Conclusion

You have joined a growing army of parents fighting the archaic practice by which school budgeting is done behind closed doors—by closed minds. Your motivation may be a sense of outrage that the schools—with all our money—have not done better by our children; or the need to defend the schools and the kids against the meat-ax approach to reducing school costs regardless of the consequences; or a glimpse into the possibility that some of our school systems (like many large organizations) have become captives of the Peter Principle—they have risen to

Illustration 34—(*Continued*)

program development." Contractual services are not a program in themselves, they provide services of many kinds. Some involve direct instruction for children (the George Washington University Workshop for Careers in the Arts, and the School Without Walls). Plans for the new Career Development program include contracts with community organizations and businesses in providing on-the-job experiences. On the basis of the "Highlights" document. Board members and citizens had no way of knowing what programs would be affected, or even eliminated, by the recommended 25% cut.

The major recommendation for redirection in FY 1972 was a cut in the number of elementary school teachers. No alternative means were presented for consideration, such as reduced or reorganized administrative staff, elimination of low-priority instructional programs, or reorganization of teaching staffs or classroom patterns. There had been no over-all review of current spending or base budget programs. Administrative divisions, such as Elementary, Secondary, and City-wide Instruction (or subject-area supervision) were listed as "programs"; no instructional program costs were given which would allow those programs to be ranked, and funded, in order of priority.

The school administration of Montgomery County, Md. prepares a pamphlet, *Choices for Our Children*, which gives somewhat more detailed information on sources of expected revenues, expected costs of maintaining a high-quality teaching staff, and a variety of proposed improvements with a specific price-tag for each. The interested citizen is given enough information to be an effective participant in the "Town Meetings" and public hearings which are held throughout the county during the budget preparation process.

In addition to the Superintendent's programs and alternatives, the proposed summary budget for the District schools should include specific information about proposed expenditures on an itemized school-by-school basis. This is the only way for citizens to determine the impact on their own schools of over-all school policy decisions. For example, if a new assistant principal for administration will be added for larger schools, exactly which schools will get one? What access will each school have to the services of reading specialists or crisis resource teachers? The Board of Education, as well as other interested people, must have this information to respond to school administration proposals.

their own level of incompetence and there they remain, entrenched. Whatever your motive, your work is *bound* to help the schools. They can use constructive, dedicated and competent help in allocating and reallocating the limited resources available to provide the vitality and excellence we desperately want for our children. And be assured that we have never met anyone who would rather do a bad job than a good job.

You know that a massive task lies ahead. You know that your success will depend primarily upon your persistence. You know that the school budget is your business.

Appendix A
Budget Review Questions*
A Checklist for your School District

1. **Policies:** Does your district have board-adopted policies governing responsibility for the budget? _____
   (*a*) Are such policies regularly reviewed and updated? _____
   (*b*) Does the board charge the superintendent with the responsiblity for initiating and directing the annual budget process? _____

2. **Planning:** Does the budget process involve long range planning? _____
   (*a*) Is there a long-range educational and financial plan adopted and updated by the school board at regular intervals? _____
   (*b*) Is there a detailed two-to-five-year plan for maintenance and repairs? _____
   (*c*) Is there a projected enrollment schedule for two-to-five years? _____
   (*d*) Is there a building and facilities construction schedule? _____

3. **Calendar:** Is there an annual budget calendar adopted by the board to identify the various budget preparation steps, insure sufficient time, and indicate who is responsible for each step? _____

4. **Equity:** Does the planning for the budget assure equitable and effective use of resources? _____
   (*a*) Is there an established per-pupil allotment for different programs, items, and expenditures? _____
   (*b*) Is there a well-planned review of all budget requests? _____

---

*This list is a modification of the budget checklist distributed by the Oregon and New York State Departments of Education.

(*c*) Are the board-approved guidelines for expenditures followed in the preparation of the budget? _____

5. **Staff Participation:** Is there a clearly defined, written budget development process that makes use of the collective knowledge and judgment of the entire staff? _____

   (*a*) Is there a staff planning and budgeting committee at each building? _____

   (*b*) Are building staff representatives included in the district-wide budgeting committee? _____

   (*c*) Does the district-wide staff budgeting committee include representatives of various interests and plan for rotation of membership? _____

   (*d*) Does the board policy designate by position the staff members who are to give leadership to the budget development process? _____

   (*e*) Are concise written instructions issued to all administrators and staff members explaining their role in budgeting? _____

6. **Citizen Participation:** Does your district have board policies that recognize the necessity and desirability of public understanding and participation? _____

   (*a*) Does your district have a planned program to use community groups and citizen participation in developing the budget? _____

   (*b*) Do citizen committees assist in the educational planning? _____

   (*c*) Does your district provide for citizen budget committees that assure some continuity in citizen participation? _____

   (*d*) Does the format of the citizen committee(s) provide for regular input and feedback with interested citizens who are not members? _____

   (*e*) Does the district have a definite method of appointing or accepting members to the citizen budget committee? Does the method provide for rotation to

assure that not all members are replaced in any single
year? _____

(*f*) Does the district have a list of powers and duties for
the budget committee? _____

(*g*) Do citizens recognize that their role is to advise and
recommend, and that the ultimate decisions are to be
made by the board? _____

(*h*) Does the citizen participation format provide citizens
with direct two-way communication with the superintendent and staff as well as with the board itself? _____

7. **Public Relations:** Does your district have a well-planned
public relations program for the budget? _____

(*a*) Is information disseminated to the community on a
year-round basis? _____

(*b*) Is the entire staff made conscious of its responsibilities for public relations regarding the budget? _____

(*c*) Does your district use special newsletters, public
meetings, newspapers, radio and television to explain
both program and financial needs regularly? _____

(*d*) Are those same channels used to provide information
about the budget, the opportunities for citizen participation in determining priorities, and sources for
additional information? _____

(*e*) Does your district distinguish between public relations and public participation—and seek to meet
both needs? _____

8. **Budget Preparation:** Does your district utilize its educational plan including goals and specific objectives in
preparing the budget? _____

(*a*) Is the budget calendar widely disseminated? _____

(*b*) Does the annual or bi-annual needs assessment for
your district involve wide participation? _____

(*c*) Have educational priorities been established with
community and staff input to the board? _____

(*d*) Does your district have an inventory of supplies and equipment? _____

(*e*) Have formulas and guidelines been adopted by the board indicating per-pupil expenditures, the pupil:teacher ratio, travel and meeting expenditures, salary schedules, merit scales, maintenance schedules, furniture and equipment guidelines, transportation and field trip guidelines? _____

(*f*) Has the staff prepared alternative revenue plans indicating potential income at various tax rates, considerations of possible legislative changes, previously untapped sources, anticipated changes in state support due to changing enrollment? _____

(*g*) Has the staff prepared alternative expenditure plans including cost effectiveness studies? _____

9. **Budget Document:** Does the budget document have the following four fundamental considerations: _____
   (*a*) An education plan? _____
   (*b*) A priority plan? _____
   (*c*) An expenditure plan? _____
   (*d*) An income plan? _____

10. Does the document contain features necessary for board, staff and community understanding? _____

   (*a*) Is there a detailed table of contents and index? _____
   (*b*) Is there a budget message? _____
   (*c*) Are there justifications for expenditures for each general category and for specific programs? _____
   (*d*) Are there explanations for any anticipated decreases or increases in revenue? _____

11. Is the budget organized by character classification including breakdown into object, function and program categories in accordance with the state accounting system of classification and further details as locally appropriate? _____

(*a*) Is there a list of expenditures by buildings? _____

(*b*) Is there a list of expenditures by department? _____.

(*c*) Is there a list of expenditures by program? _____

(*d*) Are unit costs developed for expenditures in each of the above categories? _____

12. Does the budget show the financial status of the district? Is there a schedule of bonded indebtedness? _____

(*a*) Is there a schedule of contracted salaries? _____

(*b*) Is there a schedule of contracted services, insurance, improvements? _____

(*c*) Is there a schedule of principal and interest payments for each bond issue? _____

(*d*) Are the various funds of the school district included in the annual budget document including the operating fund, the capital fund, the cafeteria fund, the transportation fund, the federal funds, the foundation funds, etc. with revenue and expenditures for each separate fund? _____

(*e*) Are fixed assets properly accounted for annually? _____

13. **Comparisons:** Does the budget document have comparisons for line items and programs? _____

(*a*) Is there an estimated expenditure for the present year to compare to the amount proposed for the forthcoming year? _____

(*b*) Is there an actual expenditure for previous years to compare to the proposed or budgeted expenditures? _____

(*c*) Is the budgeted amount for the present year available to compare with the estimated amount for the present year? _____

(*d*) Does the budget list revenues, valuations and tax rates for prior years? _____

14. **Personnel:** Does the budget document include the number and position of professional and non-professional staff related to each program or line item? _____

(a) Are comparisons included for the number of staff persons from previous years? _____

(b) Does the budget document have a detail of pupil accounting? _____

(c) Is there a census report? _____

(d) Is there an enrollment forecast? _____

(e) Is there a classroom schedule? _____

15. **Understanding:** Does the budget document itself include provisions for increasing public understanding? _____

(a) Is there a directory of names with extension numbers to be consulted for additional information regarding back-up data or explanatory material? _____

(b) Does the budget document indicate where additional copies can be obtained? _____

(c) Are several copies of the proposed, the popularized, and the adopted budget placed in the public library branches? _____

16. **Popularized Budget:** Does your school district prepare and distribute widely a popularized budget? Is it _____ distributed to all parents? to all taxpayers? to all teachers? to all staff persons? _____

(a) Does it use simple language and avoid jargon? _____

(b) Are graphs and charts utilized to show where the money comes from and where it goes? _____

(c) Does the popularized version include a brief review of the district's educational philosophy? _____

(d) Is there a list of long-range goals and immediate objectives? _____

(e) Does it describe briefly the educational program? _____

(f) Does the popularized budget point out the services, programs and activities, along with their costs, which are to be added, dropped or modified? _____

(g) Does the popularized budget provide comparative figures on a per-pupil basis within your school district as well as with comparable school districts in your state? _____

(*h*) Does it explain the basis for any substantial increase or decrease in expenditures and revenues? _____

(*i*) Is there a brief explanation of state aid and other funding mechanisms, along with the listing of anticipated receipts? _____

(*j*) Is the local tax rate explained by defining the millage and sources of local income? _____

(*k*) Does the popularized budget point out which budget needs are not being met? _____

(*l*) Is the budget calendar included in the popularized budget? _____

(*m*) Is there a listing of the dates and locations of public budget meetings in which citizens may participate, as well as the dates on board meetings? _____

(*n*) Does the popularized budget tell people where to obtain additional information? _____

(*o*) Is there a statement by the board and superintendent encouraging citizen participation in the school budget process? _____

(*p*) Is the popularized budget available in languages other than English according to local needs? _____

17. **Tentative Budget:** Does the district advertise the tentative budget along with the date and place it will meet to adopt the tentative budget? _____

(*a*) Does the board make the final decision on the content of the tentative budget? _____

(*b*) Are public explanations made and hearings held? _____

18. **Final Budget Adoption:** In fiscally dependent school districts, do the board and superintendent prepare an effective presentation of the budget to the funding body? _____

(*a*) Is public support organized and presented to the funding body in a timely and appropriate fashion? _____

(*b*) Have the funding officials been kept up to date on all budget developments throughout the year? _____

19. In districts that vote on the tax levy or budget, is the board aware of the legal options available? Is consideration given to separate votes on items which are particularly controversial? _____

(*a*) Does the board understand the possibilities and implications of successive negative votes? _____

20. Prior to final adoption, does the board publicly explain and justify all changes made since the adoption of the tentative budget? _____

21. **Budget Management:** Does the board have up-to-date written policies which provide for good internal budget controls? _____

(*a*) Is the superintendent held responsible and given the authority to implement the budget and internal control measures? _____

(*b*) Is there prompt notification to department directors and other staff members of the adopted allocation of funds for the forthcoming year? _____

(*c*) Is there a monthly balance statement of all accounts given to the board and to individual department directors? _____

(*d*) Are budget modifications or budget transfers discussed fully by the board and staff before they are authorized? _____

22. Have the budgetary procedures been evaluated to make next year's plan more effective? _____

APPENDIX B
Some Definitions

Ad Valorem Taxes: Taxes levied by a governing body on the assessed valuation of the real or personal property located within that governing body's jurisdiction.

Average Daily Attendance (ADA): The total days of pupil attendence of a given school district during a reporting period, divided by the number of days school is in session during this period.

Average Daily Membership (ADM): The sum of the days present and absent of all pupils enrolled during a reporting period divided by the number of days school is in session during this period.

Budget: A documented plan of action outlining the financial resources through which specific objectives are to be achieved.

Budgetary Transfers: After the budget for the fiscal year is finally adopted, most states permit the board of school directors to transfer funds from one line item to another, or from one program to another. Although some states specify limitations, most budgetary transfers occur quietly, by the passage by the board of resolutions that often identify only code numbers of the budgetary accounts.

Capital Outlay: An expenditure which results in the acquisition of fixed assets which are presumed to have benefits for more than one year. Examples are land, buildings, and equipment.

Chart of Accounts: A list of all accounts used in an individual accounting system. An account is a descriptive heading under which are recorded similar financial transactions.

Cost Effectiveness: An analysis designed to measure the extent to which resources allocated to a specific objective under each of several alternatives actually contribute to accomplishing that objective, so that different ways of arrival at it may be compared.

Employee Benefits: Compensation, in addition to salary, provided to an employee. This may include such benefits as health insurance, life insurance, sick leave, retirement, and social security.

Encumbrances: Purchase orders, contracts, and salary or other commitments which are chargeable to an appropriation and for which a part of the appropriation is reserved.

Functional Budget: A budget which uses the format of the line item or traditional budget to group proposed expenditures first according to general activities or actions performed. The major functional categories are: administration, instruction, pupil personnel services, pupil transportation services, health services, operation and maintenance of plant, etc., etc. Within such functions, there are additional line items for the various expenditures.

Invoice: An itemized list of merchandise purchased or services rendered from a particular seller or supplier of services. It includes quantity, description, price, terms, and date, etc.

Line Item or Traditional Budget: A budget which groups proposed expenditures according to certain categories known as the "object" of the expenditure. On each *line* of the budget, the expenses are listed just the way they are paid out: salaries on one line, supplies on another line, utilities on another line. Thus "salaries" are one object and supplies another object.

Objective: An objective is a specific description of an end result to be achieved. It should tell what (the end result), when (the target date), and who (who is accountable).

Operating Budget or **General Fund Budget:** The accounting systems of most states require that school districts keep separate records and budget separately for capital improvements (buildings, particularly). Special funds are also maintained for food service, for transportation service, for federal funds, and for other purposes in many instances. In such states, all of the other ordinary expenses are budgeted in a general fund or operating budget.

Program Budget: A program is a plan of activities or procedures design-ed to accomplish a set of related objectives. A program budget groups all the proposed expenditures for each individual program and then, within each program, the expenditures are listed according to function and object. The program budget includes the delineation or definition of the purpose or objectives of the particular program—that is, what that program is expected to accomplish. The dollar amounts budgeted are considered in relation to achieving a desired and agreed-to pur-pose.

Program budgeting differs from line-item budgeting in that it focuses on the purposes of the school district and the particular pro-gram and activity. It is a variation from the concept of functional budgeting because in the latter the budget amounts requested are mere-ly an itemization of the dollars required to continue a given activity or to install a new one. Moreover, a functional budget does not link pro-gram costs to program results.

Proposed Budget: In various states, local school districts are required to prepare a *tentative* budget and hold hearings for the public or allow the public to examine or comment on the tentative budget. This is usually called the *proposed* budget. After a prescribed period has elapsed, the school board may make changes and then adopt a final budget. It is then referred to as the *adopted* budget or, simply, the *budget*. When the school district is fiscally dependent on another municipal body, such as the town or city council, for its funds, the proposed budget is sometimes called the *budget request*. The proposed budget, or the budget request, is the one that is most hotly debated. The final budget—or the adopted budget—is the major management tool used by the administrative staff to review revenue and expen-ditures throughout the school year.

Purchase Order. A written request to a seller or vendor to supply mer-chandise or services at a given price.

Requisition: A written request to the purchasing officer for some specific service or goods. It is sent by one school official to another. Such re-quisitions are often subject to the approval of the board or superinten-dent, or representatives thereof.

Reserve for Encumbrances: An amount set aside to cover an obligation duly authorized and incurred.

Sinking Fund: Money which has been set aside or invested for the definite purpose of meeting payments on debt at some future date. It is usually a fund set up for the purpose of accumulating money over a period of years in order to have money available for the redemption of long-term obligations at the date of maturity.

Tax Budget: In those states in which the school district must request approval of a tax levy through a referendum or from another taxing body, a tentative budget is prepared called the *tax* budget. Once the amount of taxes or revenue is known, such school districts then adopt what may be called an *appropriation* budget, or a *working* budget.

Voucher: A document which authorizes the payment of money and usually indicates the account and code number to be charged in the books.

PUBLICATIONS OF NATIONAL COMMITTEE
FOR CITIZENS IN EDUCATION

PARENTS CAN UNDERSTAND TESTING—What do I.Q. and achievement tests really measure? How reliable are the results? How are tests constructed? Can tests and test results actually not be in the best interests of children? What is the future of testing in schools? These and many other key questions are discussed and answered, about tests and testing in schools, in a handbook specifically for parents. A tough controversial subject treated with clarity and competence. (**$2.50**)

COLLECTIVE BARGAINING AND TEACHER STRIKES—The Expanding Role of Parents and Citizens—When the teachers strike and the schools close, parents are uninformed spectators whereas school boards are too often unprepared for sophisticated contract negotiations. Should work contracts for public employees be modeled after private industry? Does the future hold an increased role in bargaining for parents and citizens? (*88 pages*, **$2.50**)

WHO CONTROLS THE SCHOOLS?—Who has more power to decide how children should be educated: the school board, the school administration, teacher organizations, the courts, or the federal government? Do parents and students have any power? Should they? Hard hitting, far reaching conclusions and recommendations. (*76 pages*, **$2.50**)

THE RIGHTS OF PARENTS IN THE EDUCATION OF THEIR CHILDREN—The most popular book ever published by NCCE tells parents in plain terms what rights exist under law for them and their children. The book's goal is to help parents resolve educational conflicts without going to lawyers or resorting to lawsuits. Selected as one of ten "MUST" books for 1979 by the *American School Board Journal* (*162 pages*, **$3.95**)

DEVELOPING LEADERSHIP FOR PARENT/CITIZEN GROUPS—What is "leadership"? How do you develop it in yourself and in others? How do you take the initiative? When do you assert yourself and when do you compromise? These and many other important questions about leadership development are addressed using school-oriented problems as examples. (*60 pages*, **$2.50**)

FUND RAISING BY PARENT CITIZEN GROUPS—Takes parents and citizens through the basics, from identifying sources of support to the development of a fund-raising plan. Tells how to handle follow-up and cultivate donors. Includes sample proposals, suggestions on how to form a tax-exempt organization, tips on reporting back to donors. (*52 pages*, **$2.50**)

(Continued on next page) →